YOU CAN'T STOP
MURDER

YOU CAN'T STOP
MURDER

TRUTHS ABOUT POLICING
IN BALTIMORE AND BEYOND

By Stephen Tabeling and Stephen Janis

Edited by Alan Z. Forman and Taya M. Graham

To Jerry
Steve Tabeling
10/24/20

Cover and interior design: Mike Hilton
Transcription and research: Evan Janis
Back cover photo of Stephen Janis: Dan Kempner
Back cover photo of Stephen Tabeling: Stephen Janis
Theoretical Consulting: Paul McGrew
Published by Baltimore True Crime
In association with *Voice of Baltimore*
Baltimore, MD

YOU CAN'T STOP MURDER

ACKNOWLEDGMENTS

This book is not just a chronicle of my career as a cop, but also a humble recognition of the incredible people I worked with on the cases recounted in the proceeding pages. The judges, prosecutors, and police officers listed below represent the best practitioners, protectors, and enforcers of the law I have ever met.

Each and every one of the people on this list personifies the true meaning of the term "public servant." They taught me how to be a better cop, and also how to remain a decent human being amidst the chaos and corruption that comes with investigating crime in Baltimore.

Thus I hope by acknowledging them here, I pay tribute to their service to both the community of Baltimore and the laws they fought to uphold to protect it.

The Honorable Charles E. Moylan Jr.
The Honorable Joseph Murphy
The Honorable Peter Ward
The Honorable Thomas Bollinger
The Honorable Robert Dugan
Assistant State Prosecutor Stephen R. Tully
Assistant State's Attorney Marianne Willin-Saar
Captain James J. Cadden
Major John Reintzel
Lieutenant Leander "Bunny" Nevin
Sergeant Rosario Buzzuro
Detective Steve Danko
Detective Timothy Timmons
Detective Jerome Johnson
Detective Nicholas Giangrasso
Detective Howard Corbin
Officer James Brennan
Officer Robert Holland

CONTENTS

A NOTE ABOUT THE FORMAT OF THIS BOOK

As stated above in the Acknowledgments, *You Can't Stop Murder* is not intended to simply be a chronology of my career. Instead I selected some of the most notorious cases I investigated as a jumping-off point for considering and reexamining the philosophy of policing.

Each case raises fundamental questions about the most vexing issues confronting contemporary law enforcement today. Each chapter contains both the details of the events as I recall them, along with discussion about the topic most relevant to the case itself: The law and how to apply it.

But they are also essays on the peculiarities and contradictions of trying to apply the law to people. A task that becomes even more complex when a cop confronts the most extreme types of human behavior.

In a sense this book is a detective novel, not just solely focused on the practical side of solving crimes. The enigmatic riddle I try to solve is why people commit irrational acts with regularity. To answer the question: What prompts the random act of violence, the horrible murder, the most extreme examples of human behavior? And more importantly, how should law enforcement respond? How might we endure human savagery and misbehavior and not succumb to it ourselves? And fundamentally, should there be limits to how far we as a society are willing to go to be safe?

Any good detective knows these are often the most difficult questions that populate a crime scene. After all, crime is a human endeavor, not a science or profession; we just turn it into one on the back end. And any detective will tell you, the most terrifying fact cops face while investigating a heinous crime is just how basically human it really is.

I'd also like to point out that many of the cases memorialized in this book were fairly high profile, notorious crimes. Incidents that were widely reported and the details of which are, in certain cases, contested. To construct my own history I used my collection of police reports I submitted and witness statements I recorded. To supplement these materials I also referenced a fairly healthy file of newspaper clippings from the *Baltimore Sun* and *Baltimore News American* that I saved and preserved over the years.

STEPHEN TABELING has been a cop for more than six decades, nearly half that time in Baltimore City alone, where he received 48 Commendations and six Bronze Stars for investigative work above and beyond the call of duty, retiring as a lieutenant. He began his career with the Baltimore Police Department in 1954.

Following his retirement at the end of the turbulent 1970s he served as director of public safety for Johns Hopkins Hospital and later in the same position for Loyola University Maryland (the former Loyola College) for more than a decade. In the interim he was chief of police in the City of Salisbury, on Maryland's Eastern Shore.

In 2000 Tabeling was called back by the BPD to provide an analysis of its Homicide Squad, followed by nine years of recruit training for new police officers as well as in-service training for the department's veterans.

If only it were all so simple! If only there were evil people somewhere insidiously committing evil deeds, and it were necessary only to separate them from the rest of us and destroy them. But the line dividing good and evil cuts through the heart of every human being. And who is willing to destroy a piece of his own heart?

— Aleksandr Solzhenitsyn, *The Gulag Archipelago* (1973)

CHAPTER ONE (INTRODUCTION): I NEVER WANTED TO BE A COP

Musings on Policing and the Law

I never wanted to be a cop.

In fact, growing up in East Baltimore a self-admitted trouble-maker, I hated police officers.

I was a chronic truant, a truly disinterested student who only occasionally attended St. James Elementary, a neighborhood parochial school. I skipped school so frequently my parents enlisted a city police officer to escort me to class, a task that turned out to be an exercise in futility for us all.

It's ironic that the block I grew up on is now adjacent to the site of Johnston Square Elementary School, just east of the block-wide Johnston Square Park. For a person who as a kid spent more time out of school than in, there's some poetic justice there.

My uncle was a cop also. When he visited our house at 1106 Wilcox Street, just two blocks south of Green Mount Cemetery, where John Wilkes Booth and numerous illustrious Marylanders such as Johns Hopkins and mid-twentieth century Mayor and Gov. Theodore R. McKeldin are buried, I would run out the back door and hide.

So I'm acutely conscious of the irony that I am now writing a book about my lifelong career as a police officer, particularly since the occupation I eventually embraced seemed well outside the realm of possibility, even ludicrous to the same child who grew up inventing new ways to evade the law.

It was a career that needless to say I did not plan for or even imagine, and least of all had any inkling I would ultimately grow to love.

But that's exactly what happened.

And now that I am 84 years old, having spent nearly two lifetimes wearing a badge, I have decided to write this book. Partly because I want to preserve the slice of history I witnessed investigating some of Baltimore's most notorious murder cases. Call it a compulsion of an old man who wants someone to remember what happened the day seven cops were shot on Carey Street, or when a homicidal maniac broke into City Hall with the intent to murder then-Mayor (and later Governor) William Donald Schaefer.

That's part of it.

But the other part has to do with the future — the future of policing and the state of law enforcement today, which has forced me to reexamine what it means to be a cop.

When I say reexamine it, I don't mean I have regrets. Or that I chose the wrong career. No, what I'm talking about is something entirely different: A change in how we police that has fundamentally altered what it means to put on a uniform. A departure from the basic philosophy of policing that to some extent has transformed the job I began 60 years ago into an occupation so different, I barely recognize it.

But I'm not just another old man inveighing against change. I understand that both crime and criminality evolve over time. I also understand that each new generation of law enforcement has its own unique set of challenges. However my critique of contemporary policing is not really about the way cops respond to specific crimes per se, or uniforms, or weaponry.

No, my concerns are centered upon the subtle and sometimes not so subtle shifts in the philosophy of policing that have altered every facet of what it means to be a cop. A new way of thinking, that in my opinion has fundamentally transformed what it means to wear a badge.

Call it a philosophical difference, a strategic shift, or simply a new way of thinking. But whatever it is, I don't like it.

That's why I'm writing this book. To use my experience as a Baltimore homicide investigator, a narcotics cop, and even a teacher at the city's Police Academy, to shed light on what police are doing — and not doing — and why this needs to be examined in detail.

If it sounds like an odd way to approach a book about policing, I understand. Why would a person who spent most of his life in uniform want to deconstruct the profession? Why would a man who devoted his life to enforcing the law want to unravel it in a book?

It's a good question, and a fair one. And it is one that I intend to address.

Let me say first that policing is essentially a noble profession: Upholding the law while ensuring the safety of the community is a calling unlike any other. In fact, enabling justice, protecting the unprotected, turned my career as a cop into a lifelong journey of self-improvement and education.

I can't imagine a job more satisfying than taking a violent felon or a compulsive burglar off the street. Or the innervating sense of accomplishment that accompanies slapping handcuffs on a murderer or a rapist.

But that being said, I am deeply concerned that the same occupation which gave me a sense of purpose has changed fundamentally. That in both training and emphasis, policing has been so utterly transformed by the war on drugs and the fight against terrorism that the basic mission of policing — to protect and serve — has been turned on its head. That the core set of precepts, and most importantly an adherence to the law, has been sullied by tactics that are at odds with its basic principles.

So that's why I'm writing, not just to tell a story but to hopefully teach by example. To demonstrate, through the cases I investigated and the criminals I arrested, that policing is a productive calling. That good law enforcement is not just about force, muscle, and firepower, but instead is served best by simply following the law.

Of course, my career as a cop didn't start out with such a strong sense of purpose. Truthfully, when I took the academy entrance exam back in 1952 my main concern was simply finding a job to support a growing family. Back then with just a seventh grade education my opportunities were limited. I was married with two children and a pregnant wife. Basically, I needed steady work.

But since I passed that test in 1952 and started walking the beat in Northwest Baltimore less than two years later, I have never looked back.

Since then I have worked in the trenches of the city's worst neighborhoods. I encountered my fair share of armed robbers, petty criminals, and run of the mill drug dealers. And from the first day that I stepped out of District Headquarters wearing a badge and gun belt I learned my aforementioned rebelliousness was actually an asset on the rough-hewn streets of Baltimore.

But that's not all, because along with the realization that a rough and tumble youth could turn into a pretty effective street cop, came another, more interesting discovery that defined my career. It was a slow, substantive comprehension that drove me to delve deep into the one aspect of law enforcement that every cop should know, embrace, and of course understand.

The importance of the law.

It may sound naïve, obvious, or simply dumb. Hard to believe my grand revelation about the occupation of policing was that it's all about the law. That understanding the law is the first thing a cop should learn before he straps on a gun belt. I mean, what else are police but the human enforcers of the law?

Still, as simple as that sounds, it's quite an easy idea to forget — and I'm afraid we have. It's easy to dismiss the law, working the violent streets of Baltimore where your marching orders are to disrupt a corner-full of drugs dealers, when your effectiveness is measured simply by how many people you put in jail.

It's easy to forget when you're fighting something called the "war on drugs," with a policy called "zero tolerance," working in a unit called a "tactical squad" trained in techniques developed on the battlefields of Iraq. It's even easier when you're chasing shadowy terrorists herding bombs in nondescript minivans toward a hundred-story tower — to justify tapping a cellphone without a warrant.

Call it modernization or militarization or any other clever name you want, these are the buzzwords that define policing today, and I don't think much of it. Mostly because it has very little to do with enforcing the law, far more to do with politics. Extreme philosophies of enforcement that have changed policing for the worse.

That's why I want to share with future generations my lifetime experience as a cop. I want to make the case that policing needs to change, that law enforcement needs an overhaul, that being a cop must evolve into something different.

Let's face it: we have more people in prison than any country in the world. We have layer upon layer of law enforcement with ever-expanding bureaucracies to administer it, and more political patrons to protect it. It's an industry unto itself that has become rarified, politicized, and even anesthetized to its original purpose.

So in order to demonstrate how out of kilter policing is, I'm going to make a point that may seem radical, something which completely contradicts the pervasive perception of what the law means to cops. It will also demonstrate that the idea that the law is an obstacle, impediment, or detriment to policing is false.

Put simply, it's crap. Let me give you an example: The Baltimore City Police. (That's right, my department.)

It's an agency I served, and respect. It's an organization that provided me a decent living and an exciting career. An agency that took a man with only a seventh grade education and gave him a respectable job. And a department with help from the Law Enforcement Assistance Administration which allowed me to obtain a Bachelor of Arts Degree and an M.A. in psychology, plus several advanced certificates from Loyola University. So I have both admiration and respect as well as a deep sense of gratitude toward the Baltimore Police Department.

But recently the BPD has been rocked with a series of stunning scandals. Mishaps and bad behavior I would argue stem from a lack of respect for and true comprehension of the law.

From the indictment and conviction of 17 officers who took bribes for directing accident victims to a crooked towing company, to officers actively discouraging rape victims from reporting sexual assaults, the department has demonstrated a lack of organizational integrity that I believe has much to do with not grasping the laws that define policing.

Take an officer named Gahiji Tshamba.

After a night of drinking at a midtown bar, he shot and killed an unarmed former U.S. Marine in an alley, pumping 12 bullets into the Iraq War veteran because he flirted with Tshamba's girlfriend by patting her on the behind. The case drew national attention because Tshamba's weapon reached what is known as lock-back, the point where the firing mechanism locks because an entire clip has been expended. It was unconscionable overkill that sent Tshamba to jail for 15 years after a judge chastised him for savagery.

Or the shooting of Officer William Torbit, killed by four fellow cops outside a nightclub called the Select Lounge during a mass of confusion and poor supervision in handling an after-hours crowd.

And recently a firearms trainer at the Police Academy actually shot a trainee in the head during a training exercise. Seriously, an experienced academy trainer brought a live firearm into what's known as Simunition Training. That is, training using only simulated ammunition weapons. It was a basic and fundamental mistake that could never have happened if the rules had been followed. But they weren't, and as a result, a handicapped former police cadet now faces a life of rehab and limited mobility.

These are just a small sampling of the miscues, misdeeds, and misbehavior that have plagued the department over the past few years. But the real scandal, the most costly collective act of malfeasance, which has received less attention, is actually a clearer-cut example of why cops need to know the law. A policy that shows the law actually protects cops too.

ZERO TOLERANCE

I'm referring to the strategy called "zero tolerance." A plan which called for thousands of quality-of-life arrests in violent neighborhoods to curtail more serious crime. A new way to combat violence by simply locking people up for petty infractions such as drinking beer on a stoop or "expectorating"... also known as spitting.

But it spun out of control.

In 2005, for example, the department made 110,000 documented arrests. That's one arrest for every six residents in the city. But in reality Baltimore's experiment with zero tolerance led to tens of thousands of illegal arrests of poor and often black residents of the city.

During its heyday officers were often called "Jump-Out Boys," because cops would descend in vans into a neighborhood, and literally jump out, in the process arresting every black male they could find.

It was also a policy which prompted the NAACP and ACLU to sue, a lawsuit which led to a million-dollar settlement. It was a settlement that acknowledged the department targeted poor, minority neighborhoods and willfully engaged in illegal arrests as a matter of policy. A policy which left thousands of young men with criminal records, regularly filled the city's primary jail beyond capacity, and left the police department tainted for misusing the power of arrest to maintain a semblance of order.

And like all the examples I've mentioned thus far, the policy of zero tolerance is much easier to define by what it wasn't: lawful. The entire fiasco of the zero tolerance strategy is premised upon an idea that has nothing to do with law enforcement, because it was not legal.

Let me be blunt: There is absolutely no legal authority in the U.S. Constitution to detain people without probable cause. There has never been or likely ever will be a law that allows police to march black people into the back of a van simply because they were assembling. So long as the Constitution of the United States and the Bill of Rights are the law of the land, Baltimore's entire policy of zero tolerance was predicated upon an illegal premise.

In fact, it was such a flagrant misuse of police powers that I am truly surprised no federal agency ever stepped in.

I remember the line made famous by New York City Police Officer Frank Serpico. He was an honest cop who exposed bribe-taking and payoffs inside the New York City Police Department when he testified against police corruption in 1971. During testimony in front of a special commission, Serpico made a semantic distinction that still resonates four decades later:

There is no such thing as a crooked cop... just crooks, and cops.

So, taking that distinction a step further, an agency that doesn't follow the law cannot be a true enforcer of the law. And when that agency admits de facto that a policy which was systemically implemented over a prolonged period of time is illegal, well, I think you see my point.

But how, you ask, can a police department wholly and willfully run afoul of the law? How can a law enforcement agency implement an unlawful policy? And how can officers themselves continue to execute policies so completely and consistently unlawful?

Well, it's easy if the officers who work in the agency have a less than complete knowledge of the law.

Let me explain.

THE FOURTH, FIFTH AND SIXTH AMENDMENTS

After I retired I was asked by former Police Commissioner Leonard Hamm to teach the law to cops at the city's education and training facility, otherwise known as the Police Academy. In the early part of the last decade the department had reduced the time devoted to teaching the law for reasons unknown to me, and Commissioner Hamm wanted to revive the curriculum.

So I accepted the job because, as you already know, I am passionate about teaching the law to cops.

The first couple of classes I taught focused on so-called in-service training, a refresher course on the basics of constitutional law for frontline supervisors, primarily sergeants and lieutenants. The idea was to make sure the department's middle management was familiar with the basic laws which govern what cops can and cannot do.

Bear in mind, the Fourth, Fifth and Sixth Amendments to the Constitution define policing.

The Fourth Amendment is the source of police powers: it governs how we conduct searches and obtain evidence and even when we can make an arrest.

The Fifth Amendment dictates under what circumstances we can question a suspect. It's also the source of the concept known as Miranda rights, the now-famous legal precedent which requires cops to inform suspects that they have the right not to incriminate themselves, to protect themselves from being prosecuted for something they might say under questioning.

And the Sixth Amendment is equally important because it sets out what can and cannot occur during a criminal trial, a set of precepts that extend beyond the courtroom and dictate how we gather evidence.

All of these legal ideas form the basis of American policing. Each sets forth useful protocols and standards of conduct which make a cop more effective, efficient, and productive. Remember, these laws weren't really designed to help cops. The fundamental idea was to protect the innocent, to keep us free, a legal imperative we too often take for granted.

Think, in a country with an increasingly powerful contingent of police agencies, federal law enforcement, and even homeland security, how on earth does an innocent individual stand a chance? How can anyone truly remain free while the powers of governmental agencies become broader and more far-reaching? Who can fight back against a federal government with unlimited resources to investigate, detain, and prosecute?

That's the genius of the presumption of innocence: it puts the onus on the government to prove guilt, a simple, logical and effective legal restraint. From that starting point, checks and balances naturally emerge because the burden of proof is designed to be just that — a burden. It's that burden supplemented by reasonable limits on what cops can and cannot do to meet it which makes for better policing and freer civilians.

So the first thing I did with each class was to give the students an assessment test on the Fourth, Fifth and Sixth Amendments. It was a quick half-hour quiz to get a feel for what they knew, and what they needed to know, about critical parts of the Constitution.

I asked a series of basic questions:

How does the Fourth Amendment grant arrest authority? What is the meaning of probable cause? What is the meaning of reasonable suspicion?

Regarding the Fifth Amendment, I asked them to outline the differences between custodial interrogation and non-custodial interrogation.

And for the Sixth Amendment, I sought a simple delineation of when a suspect has the right to an attorney. I also asked them to enumerate any scenario when you can talk to a defendant without the presence of an attorney.

These are all crucial questions that govern the basic procedures of policing and investigation.

To stop an automobile and search it, or to arrest a suspect when you've witnessed a crime, is when a cop needs the powers granted in the Fourth Amendment. Custodial and non-custodial interrogation is a crucial distinction enumerated in the Fifth, defining when and how you can detain someone during an investigation. And the Sixth Amendment question is one of the most crucial of all: What are the implications of those aforementioned powers? When can you detain a suspect and ask questions? as opposed to When are you simply "talking"?

Bottom line, these three brief amendments strike a delicate balance between our individual freedom and the enforcement of the law. It's a principled division of powers that attempts to give cops the ability to do their job within reasonable limits.

And knowing and understanding these limits is essential to being a good cop. They offer not just obstacles, but opportunities.

Take for example the recent debate about the timing of Mirandizing the Boston Marathon bomber, Dzhokhar Tsarnaev. As I mentioned before, reading a suspect his or her Miranda rights is a prerequisite for asking questions to obtain court-admissible evidence.

The concern, mostly misinformed, was that police would not be able to get any information out of Tsarnaev after he was thus advised. It was a debate that raged for days, a completely ridiculous discussion which hinged upon a faulty premise. Because any cop well-versed in the Constitution would understand what I already related about Mirandizing: it is only necessary if you plan to use a suspect's statements as evidence against him.

In other words, you can talk all day long if you don't need what the suspect says to prove the case in court. Simply put, if you have enough proof he or she committed a crime, then Miranda is merely an afterthought.

In Tsarnaev's case, there appeared to be more than enough evidence to win a conviction without a single statement from him. He was captured on video at the Boston Marathon shortly before the bombings occurred. Images taken at the scene showed him placing a backpack on the ground where the first bomb exploded and then casually walking away as the mayhem unfolded around him.

So in his case Miranda becomes irrelevant. You can ask him anything, you just can't use his answers in court. The point is, an investigator trained in the law knows and uses that knowledge to his or her advantage.

But back to my test.

The test results were deplorable. Some questions were answered completely incorrectly. Many responses showed a total lack of understanding of the law. Truthfully a majority of both sergeants and lieutenants, the mainstay of the BPD's supervisory ranks, could not adequately answer basic questions about the U.S. Constitution. Not a single cop I taught during a three-year stint at the academy had a full and complete understanding at the out-set of basic constitutional concepts.

In other words they knew next to nothing about the laws that defined their jobs. Even worse, they knew virtually nothing about what actually empowered them to be cops. It was like dealing with an auto mechanic who can't identify a carburetor or a doctor without a rudimentary knowledge of anatomy.

It was a disaster, but also quite revealing.

Because whether it's illegal activity by individual cops or a policy like zero tolerance, it's a hell of a lot easier for law enforcement to turn bad if the law itself is a mystery to the people in uniform who are sworn to enforce it. But not only that, it's much easier to turn a police department into an instrument of politics with policies like zero tolerance if the majority of officers don't understand basic legal concepts.

I'm sure you think this sounds naïve or even like wishful thinking, but knowledge of the law actually empowers an officer. Once a cop understands it, and how much sense it makes, it's harder to implement policies like zero tolerance simply because the law becomes ingrained in him or her, even habitual.

In fact, nothing is more important to training an effective police officer than teaching a working respect for the Constitution. It provides a sense of purpose and mission that is difficult to shake.

As I used to remind the students in my academy classes, the work they do on the street could well end up in front of the U.S. Supreme Court. Many a car stop, or routine arrest, or search by a patrol officer has landed on the docket of the highest court in the country, and that makes the job of each and every beat cop vitally important beyond simply controlling crime.

They are in fact the practical appliers of the law of the land.

So when I teach officers about the basic constitutional precepts, it actually becomes a process of empowerment.

They learn that enforcing the law is not just about chasing suspects in back alleys and making drug busts, but preserving the basic and fundamental concepts that make American democracy uniquely vibrant. It turns the sometimes unglamorous work of a patrol officer or a beat cop into a calling. And even more important, lays the groundwork for the habits and practices of a good investigator.

Which is the major reason why I'm writing this book: to revel in the potency of the law. Not as a blunt instrument for incarcerating poor people, but as a means of maintaining a civil society through good policing. Not as a bludgeon for the civil rights-averse drug warriors, but as a tool to deter bad behavior and remove bad actors from the community.

Because in the trenches of one of the most violent cities in the country, it's all you've got. When a vigilante group is meting out street justice, the law is what keeps cops from confronting vengeance with indiscriminate violence. When a city awash in drugs tries to fight back, the law ensures police actually weed out the bad apples while keeping the community intact.

The funny thing about the law is, it works. Zero tolerance was a bust. At its height, the homicide rate in the city actually climbed higher. Only when then-Mayor Sheila Dixon abandoned the strategy in 2007 and shifted to targeted enforcement, focusing on the worst of the worst, did the city's homicide rate begin to decline.

Mass illegal arrests were shown to be not just illegal, but bad policy.

But enough ink on extolling the virtues of the law; this book is about showing how it actually works on the streets. It's about real cases: life and death scenarios, murders and murderers. It will reveal that if the law is applied correctly, police can do good work. In fact, the law properly applied is an instrument of creativity wrought by reason. Without it, our freedoms would vanish. With it, cops can and should fight to preserve it.

In Aleksandr Solzhenitsyn's book, *The Gulag Archipelago*, he writes of the dozens of forced labor camps spawned by the Communist Party during the rise of the Soviet Union. Known as "gulags," he argues that the growth of the oppressive Bolshevik government was fueled and supported by mass imprisonment bolstered by the unchecked power to detain. The first chapter is titled simply, "Arrest." In it he enumerates all the unconstitutional techniques that allowed Soviet authorities to arrest tens of thousands of people, an incarceration which transformed citizens into slaves with little hope of ever being released.

It's an eye-opening read, because it seems so foreign, so removed — and yet not. Could you imagine the U.S. Government detaining people in such an arbitrary manner? Or fathom your own local law enforcement agency imprisoning tens of thousands of innocent people based upon a dangerous and ultimately dysfunctional political imperative? Who would think in our country policing could be twisted to use arrests at the behest of political ambition?

Well, what about zero tolerance? What about the tens of thousands of people we illegally arrested in Baltimore? People who were imprisoned to the tune of 150 bucks per day, courtesy of the city's taxpayers? Prisoners who ultimately made every piece of furniture that sits in public university classrooms around the state, all for the maximum wage of several dollars a day?

It's another reason why I'm writing this book. To preserve the history of the cases I worked, with the hope it can inform the present. To argue forcefully through the lessons of the past that policing is a preoccupation that merits fierce debate and constant rethinking. To continue a fight to maintain the purpose and integrity of the law so that future generations might enjoy its benefits unimpeded.

Bottom line, we are a nation that values freedom above all else, and we need to constantly rework the philosophy of policing to balance that idea against the burgeoning powers of law enforcement.

Put simply, the job of police is to respect the law — by defending it.

We also have to remember that law enforcement is a complex process fraught with the opportunity to protect as well as imperil. It's a process that should sit at the crossroads of politics, but not on any particular side. That's why the law exists, to keep both cops and civilians safe and free.

But it's an ongoing battle with plenty of gray area. The struggle between law enforcement and our inviolable liberties requires constant vigilance and thoughtful adjustment. It's really a process of thinking about how we want to live between freedom and the law.

As an old, retired cop, I hope I can show you how the twain can meet on equal ground and thrive to benefit us all.

CHAPTER TWO:
YOU CAN'T STOP MURDER

The Good Friday Massacre

You can't stop murder.

You can solve it, even study it. But the truth is you can't stop it.

If someone really wants to kill, they will. If they're dead set on murder, they'll find a way.

Think about it: how would you stop a murder before it happens? What I mean is, how would you prevent murder?

Become a mind reader? hire a psychic? Put a cop on every corner? and a camera in every home? Put every young man between the ages of 18 and 30 under surveillance simply because they're the demographic most likely to kill?

You could do all these things and more, and maybe, just maybe you'd actually prevent a few killings. You might even get lucky and stop a senseless mass murder. But in the end, all the resources and time you expend won't add up. The few lives you might save won't even come close to justifying the massive dedication of time and resources.

So, given this dilemma, let me rephrase the question: Is murder preventable?

The question is, of course, purposely provocative, and maybe even absurd. It's meant to make you think. Think about murder like a cop. Because when people murder, we, the cops, get the call. The most extreme act of human violence is our problem, as it should be... to a degree.

My job for nearly a decade was to solve murders, catch killers. When I worked in the Baltimore City Homicide Department, our clearance rate, the number of cases we solved, averaged in excess of 90 percent. Not a bad track record in a city that notched upwards of 300 killings a year. And that's how we were judged, by our clearance rate. It was our benchmark for success or failure. How many cases we solved.

But not anymore.

Crime stats in Baltimore and other major cities have been politicized. Numbers like the homicide rate are not just a tally of the dead. They're all-important barometers of cities' health, benchmarks of political success. A signal that a city is safe, that business is good, and that real estate is worth buying.

Many a political career in Baltimore has been predicated on reducing crime, at least statistically. Presidential aspirant and former Mayor of Baltimore Martin O'Malley staked his career on attempting to lower the homicide rate below 200, a goal he never achieved.

But it was this fusing of politics to crime stats that changed how a police department is evaluated, and as a result, how we policed. It led to pressure to control crime in a way that was unprecedented, with specialized units and run-and-gun tactics, aggressive zero tolerance arrests — and skirting the law.

All predicated upon the idea that murder can be prevented, and that cops are the cure.

What worries me now after nearly 60 years of being a cop, are the unseen consequences of this philosophical shift. No one ever asks if this idea makes sense. No one really thinks about the implications of equating tougher laws, increased policing... with safety.

When I was working homicide we believed the best way to prevent future murders was to close the cases of the present. That's how we were trained. From our perspective, taking a killer off the streets "solves" all the murders he didn't have the freedom to commit.

But now the homicide clearance rate averages between 40–60 percent. The Homicide Unit, which I analyzed in 2000 for then-Commissioner Ed Norris, is staffed with fewer experienced officers than ever.

It seems, at least to me, then and now, the belief that we can prevent murders puts less emphasis on solving them.

And so the original question still remains: Can murder be prevented? Can you actually stop someone from picking up a gun, and killing? Better put, could you stop a murderer, who gave you advance warning?

What if a killer actually called homicide on the phone, said "I'm going to kill someone," and even offered up a rough idea of how he was going to do it? What if this killer even revealed a somewhat vague, albeit helpful, time and place when the killing would occur? And what if this same sociopath even took the time to describe the weapons and ammo he had at his disposal? With all these details, it would be easy to stop him, right? Piece of cake, right?

And if you couldn't stop him, what does this say about this murky belief that cops can prevent human beings from behaving badly?

Because in 1976, that's exactly what happened. We did indeed get a call from a killer, a killer who told us in no uncertain terms what he was going to do, and when he was going to do it. But what happened says quite a bit about the limits of policing, and what we might want to consider when we debate how to stop today's murderers.

A CRYPTIC CALL

It was April 16, 1976, Good Friday, when a call came in to the homicide floor from a man who said he was going kill people.

Lots of them.

I had just finished a 48-hour shift investigating a murderous rampage at City Hall. A crazed gunman stalked the corridors of the temporary headquarters for city government in search of the mayor.

A disgruntled restaurant owner, angry that the city Health Department had shut down his carryout business, was looking to settle a beef with then-Mayor William Donald Schaefer, at the end of the barrel of a gun.

Fortunately, a quick-thinking office manager barricaded the mayor's office and told the disgruntled restaurateur the mayor was in Annapolis, which was true.

But unfortunately, the man took out his anger on several council members, shooting and killing Councilman Dominic Leone and wounding Councilman Carroll Fitzgerald. The stress of seeing Leone lying on the floor dying caused Councilman Joseph Curran Sr. to suffer a heart attack from which he never recovered. Curran died a year later.

I'll talk more about that case in due course, but needless to say we had to have a detailed report on the desk of then-Commissioner Donald Pomerleau pronto, which is why I literally hadn't slept in two days after the shooting occurred.

But within a couple hours of arriving home I got a call from one of my detectives. "Sir," he said, "I think we have a problem."

"Really," I replied, hardly able to concentrate. "What kind of problem?"

"A guy just called and said he was going to kill people, lots of people."

I didn't respond at first; I was tired, worn out, and stressed. I mean, we had just dealt with the murder of a councilman inside City Hall.

And now this?

But even through the haze of a 48-hour stretch without sleep, I thought back to my training, my street experience, the things I learned before I became a cop.

Holidays are tough, particularly for nutcases. And it was Good Friday. So I asked: "What did he say?"

The caller was male, young, perhaps in his twenties, the detective told me. He talked quickly, like he was in a hurry. The detective could hear traffic, like the caller was talking from a payphone.

"I'm going to kill some people and hurt anyone who gets in my way," the caller said.

"Why?" the detective asked him.

"I can't get a job, my foster father hates me, and my girlfriend just left me."

"But why take out your problems on innocent people?" the detective countered.

That's when the detective told me the speaker's voice turned calm, resolute. As if the act of simply airing his grievances, and what he was planning to do to right them, was enervating.

"No one cares about me... so why should I have feelings towards them?" he asked.

He then proceeded to explain in exacting detail what he intended to do.

He planned to start shooting as soon as it got dark. He had high-powered weapons, he said, lots of ammo, and was a trained shooter. He had been planning a massacre for two weeks.

As the conversation continued, the detective tried to draw him out, extract a few bits of information. He wouldn't give up any clues to his whereabouts, or identity, but what he did tell us, was not good.

He told the detective he was going to kill his foster father and an ex-girlfriend named "Joyce."

He said he had been sniffing ignition spray regularly since he was 15 and had occasionally used LSD. He said the world was different when he was high; that it was the only time when things "looked good."

He said he enjoyed shooting, had joined the Army, but had been discharged against his will. He also said he had been arrested for larceny and handgun possession. He then offered a tantalizing clue: he lived in the vicinity of Lombard and Monroe Streets.

And then the really bad news: He was well-armed. This angry young man told the detective he had access to an 8-millimeter rifle, 200 rounds of 240-grain ammunition, and several shot-guns. He ended the conversation with a single, prophetic threat:

"I'm going to kill cops too." And then he hung up.

I didn't hesitate; as I said before, it was a holiday, and holidays bring out the worst in people both sane and insane alike.

So I directed the detective to send out a citywide bulletin with specific instructions: "Be aware, and on the lookout in the vicin-ity of Lombard and Monroe Streets." I also instructed him to relay as much detailed information about the content of the phone call as possible.

And then I hung up and waited.

I couldn't sleep. Despite being exhausted, I was in fact restless, lying in bed wide awake.

Yes, people call the BPD and make threats every day, the major-ity of which turn out to be bogus. You'd be surprised how often nut-jobs call police and recount plans to kill their mother or to blow something up.

But this guy was different, this guy seemed serious. He was detailed, exacting, and calm, according to my detective. He was prepared, equipped, and angry. And even more troubling, he had a motive.

Not a motive that made sense to me, or any other sane person for that matter. But a motive with enough impulsive sociopathic logic for us to take his threats seriously. Personal failures height-ened by a sense of social isolation. A feeling of impotence inten-sified by a lack of personal responsibility. Put simply, he blamed the world for his problems, not himself... and so the world was going to pay for it.

And indeed it did.

THE FIRST SHOT

Lombard and Carey Streets are pretty much the same today as they were on the evening of April 16, 1976.

Hard scrabble row homes, then owned by blue-collar Baltimoreans, stretching for blocks. The abandoned B & O Railroad yard lingering like an unmarked grave to the west. A steady stream of automobile traffic, headed east toward the city center. The only difference between then and now, packs of sleepwalking junkies who crowd the sidewalks, patrons of a nearby methadone clinic.

On that Good Friday evening though, the neighborhood was crawling with cops, tactical units and patrol cars. Specialized units and regular patrols cruising neighborhoods in the vicinity of Lombard and Monroe Streets in search of a potential killer.

As I said before and after, I made sure the homicide unit took the threat seriously. My detective shared what little we knew with the rest of the department. Thus we had plenty of boots on the ground.

Still, our state of preparedness didn't amount to much. I mean, we were ready, we had time to prepare. We could saddle up and rally the troops. We even had a proximate location. And of course, we had more guns than he did.

But in the end, it still didn't matter.

The first shot hit a K-9 car. A bullet fired from somewhere near the corner of Lombard and Carey Streets that careened off the hood. The sound of the volley caught the attention of one of the tactical units in the area, which quickly responded.

Cops began to swarm the corner of Carey and Lombard. Detectives, streets cops, and even a specialized unit arrived on the scene as the sniper unleashed a fusillade of hollow-point bullets.

The unknown shooter was indeed capable, firing off rounds in quick succession as cops descended on the area. Volleys so intense, officers later said they could barely find cover, let alone shoot back. Cops found themselves taking cover in place. Bullets were flying, civilians caught on the street were in a state of panic.

Tactically speaking it was a worst of both worlds scenario, cops unsure of where to shoot, fighting an expert marksman on higher ground and with better cover. "Advise them not to come up Carey Street," an officer on the scene radioed to a dispatcher. "They're going to get shot."

"Keep them off Lombard," another officer relayed.

As more officers poured into the area from surrounding districts, bits and pieces of information from men on the scene also started to trickle in, all of it bad.

"Information from neighbors: this guy's got an arsenal in there," one officer warned.

"The subject is armed with a high-powered sniper rifle; stay out of the unit block of Carey Street," another officer relayed from the scene.

Still, during the initial onslaught, Baltimore's Finest fought back.

One officer bravely positioned his car on Carey Street directly in the line of fire in an attempt to get the exact location of the shooter. Another ran down Lombard Street as bullets whizzed by his ear, attempting to move a group of residents who had gathered on a nearby corner in the line of fire.

Several cops took cover behind a car parked directly across the street near the Engine 13 Firehouse on Carey Street, valiantly trading shots with the gunman.

Among them, a cop named Jimmy Holcombe, just 31 years old.

According to reports he was one of the first cops on the scene, quickly taking and giving fire from behind a parked car. Tragically however, Holcombe was shot in the upper throat and chest, a mortal wound.

But even as he lay dying on the sidewalk, firefighters risked their own lives to treat his wounds. It was, to say the least, a war zone.

As the bullets continued to rain down on Lombard Street, calls to dispatchers described a frantic battle to stay alive, and treat the wounded.

"My partner's hit, get an ambo," radioed one officer.

Several tactical officers were ordered to storm 1303 West Lombard Street from the rear, the row home near Carey Street where the shooter was apparently holed up. But when the group sidled near a back door, they were greeted with a vicious blast of shotgun pellets, a volley fired from a rear third-floor window that gravely wounded two officers and left the others scrambling for cover.

Amidst the chaos, there were miraculous acts of bravery too, and not just by the cops.

Two civilians volunteered to drive Detective Nicholas Giangrasso into the line of fire to evacuate an injured officer with their own van. As they stormed around the corner of Carey Street, bullets clipped the vehicle, busting out a rear window. Still, the two kept driving, offering cover to the detective as he quickly dragged the injured cop into the back of the van before they sped off down Lombard for the hospital. One by one, many of the cops bravely shot back at the well-armed sniper with their .38-caliber service revolvers.

One by one, those same cops were hit. In fact, the northeast corner of Carey Street was, simply put, a bloodbath: a cop blood bath. Which is exactly what I saw when I first arrived at the scene... blood and chaos.

I can't remember exactly who I spoke to first, but I do remember being so utterly mortified by the carnage that I pushed an unsuspecting officer up against a wall on the south side of Lombard

Street: "I need you to tell me right now what the hell is going on here," I yelled at the bewildered officer.

The answer wasn't pretty. We were pinned down. The blocks surrounding the intersection of Carey and Lombard were all under constant attack. Even with dozens of cops now taking and returning fire from every possible angle we weren't able to get a good shot at the sniper.

In fact, even though we'd narrowed down the position of the shooter to a third-floor window of 1303 West Lombard, our snipers still couldn't get a clear read on him. "He's moved to the rear of the third floor again," a police sniper told a dispatcher as he tried to zero in. And while we struggled, the bullets kept flying. True to his word, the marksman was hitting his mark, and using the storehouse of weaponry he bragged about on the phone.

In all my years as a cop I don't think I've ever witnessed such an intense gun battle. Never had I seen so many cops hurt, so much firepower directed by one person with such exacting results. It was a mess of epic proportions.

And then, what happened next, was a miracle.

The shooter did something totally unexpected, a decision that turned one of my most violent days as a cop, into one of the weirdest.

Because the same vicious, unrelenting sniper that picked off cops like carnival targets, for reasons unknown, did something even more unpredictable and unexpected than picking up a gun in the first place.

He called us on the phone.

I'm not kidding. The kid simply walked down the stairs to the basement of 1303 West Lombard, picked up a rotary telephone, and dialed 911.

A young man whose name we would soon learn was John Earl Williams, the Good Friday Shooter, was apparently scared.

"Listen, they're shooting at me," he complained to a seemingly clueless 911 operator.

"Who's shooting at you?" the dispatcher asked.

"The police."

"Where are you?"

"I'm the person at 1303, just tell 'em I'm coming out, just don't shoot me!" he implored.

"Oh come on," the operator replied, apparently incredulous.

"I'm not playing, miss."

After a few minutes of more obtuse exchanges, the befuddled dispatcher handed the phone to a supervisor, who luckily seemed to know what was going on.

"Call 'em up, just do anything; tell 'em to quit shooting at me, I'm coming out of the house peacefully," Williams yelled into the phone.

"You're coming out peacefully?" the supervisor replied.

"Yes, they're shooting at me because I was firing back, but I'm going to surrender. I'm giving up, but they won't listen to me."

After several more minutes of convincing Williams he wasn't going to get shot, the supervisor gave him specific instructions:

"All right John, go ahead out. Put your hands in the air."

"Please don't tell me a lie, I don't want to get shot!"

"They won't shoot you. You got my word, they won't shoot you."

Eventually, Williams agreed to walk out the door, hands in the air. That was the plan, walk out peacefully. I would cuff him and that would be that, it would all be over.

Almost.

Because I realized as I stood outside that now infamous row home on Lombard Street, the suspect who was about to emerge was as good as dead. I mean he had just shot seven cops, killing one. His current life expectancy would be measured in footsteps, literally the number of seconds it would take him to exit the house and stand on the stoop. He was the most marked man in Baltimore City history.

Which is why when he finally walked out the door, I was taken aback.

Because the man standing in the hallway, the crazed killer who had rained bullets down on the largest collection of cops in the city's history, the merciless sniper who had gunned down seven police officers, the murderous psychopath who had single-handedly drawn half the goddam city police force to South Baltimore was a small, unassuming teen.

A tiny kid wearing horned-rimmed glasses, shaking like a leaf. A punk who a few minutes before was ruthlessly gunning down cops, and now begging for his life.

So for a few seconds I just kind of stood there gaping at this mass of physical contradictions standing in the doorway. How, I wondered, did a freaking child create this big a mess?

But before I could even get near Williams, two other cops beat me to the punch, literally. An angry cop greeted Williams with a stiff uppercut to the nose, the opening salvo in what appeared to be a serious beat-down in the making. I had to use my most authoritative lieutenant's voice to squelch it.

"Hand him over now!" I barked. "Now!"

Then I simply grabbed the suspect by the arm and dragged him into a waiting patrol car. And just for the record, I understand the sentiment. The son-of-a-bitch kid was a cop killer.

He wounded more police officers in 30 minutes than I'd ever witnessed. He shot at cops and civilians taking cover. He was, put simply, a monstrous coward. But the law is the law. As cops, we enforce, we don't adjudicate. Street justice and civilization don't mix. If vengeance gets the upper hand, things fall apart quickly. The job of a cop is to arrest, not to punish. You can't use a badge to settle scores, no matter how much the crime seems to justify it.

Still, as the patrol car pulled away from the curb with 18-year-old John Earl Williams in the backseat, I was in a slight state of shock. It was just difficult to reconcile the tiny kid with the mayhem I had just witnessed. A life and death struggle all predicated on the whim of a boy. A child really, who had just unleashed a savage unrelenting attack on people he didn't know, and in the process, killed a cop.

But as I struggled with the absurdity of this murderous man-boy, I also began to prepare for the postscript. Steeling myself for the most tedious part of police work, the part that rarely gets any attention, the practical details of cleaning up a mess, even as adrenaline still courses through your veins.

Because as the patrol car pulled away, I knew that just like the report I had completed a mere 12 hours earlier on the shooting at City Hall, the powers that be would want a fully detailed write-up on the evening's events on their desk within a matter of days.

That's right, days.

For the record, down at Homicide, Williams told the same sob story he had recounted to my detective. He said he was depressed about his breakup with Joyce, adding that when it got dark he simply climbed to the third floor of the row home he shared with his mother and starting shooting.

He claimed he had not intended to hurt anyone, but that when the police arrived, he got scared. He said he shot at them to keep them from shooting at him. To deliver this message of peace Williams told detectives he used a .300-magnum rifle, a shotgun, and an 8-millimeter rifle.

Investigators also spoke to Joyce, the 15-year-old girl who was apparently the focus of Williams' ire. She told them she had indeed broken up with Williams. He was crazy, she said. In fact, she spoke to him just before the shooting. He told her the police would soon be at his house and he would shoot "anyone who got in the way."

Her reply was succinct: "You don't have the guts to do it."

He then left a cryptic note with her mother. "Some people can only go so long before they go crazy. I'm almost there."

So there were warning signs. Pretty obvious red flags. But if no one cares, who will read them?

Still, as I said before, it was my job to clean up... and quick.

A crime scene is like a puzzle, except the pieces are scattered where you're least likely to look. Bullets have to be located, weapons confiscated and catalogued. Fingerprints found on casings, scraps of paper with illegible notes, bagged and numbered for evidence control.

But it wasn't just latent clues we were after. We already knew the basics, the who, what, where and when. We were most interested in the why and how.

We were looking for guns. And they weren't hard to find.

The row home Williams shared with his mother was a veritable armory. There were guns everywhere, and I mean in every nook and cranny in the house.

On the second floor in his mother's room we found a .300-magnum rifle, a 12-gauge shotgun, and two .22-caliber rifles. We also found a .30-06 rifle, another 12-gauge shotgun hidden in a closet, and loaded .22-magnum and a .38-caliber revolver stuffed in a dresser drawer.

Worse yet, the so-called Saturday Night Special .38 was listed in our database as stolen.

On the third floor where Williams did most of the shooting, it looked like a gun club run amok. We found four rifles in that room alone: a Winchester .30-30 with a scope, a Danzie 8-millimeter, a Remington Model 700, and a .200 Winchester magnum augmented with a scope. In a back room we also discovered a Westfield m550 shotgun, the weapon Williams used to ambush the officers who tried to enter his home from the alley.

It was, to say the least, an impressive array of weaponry.

And there was the ammo. Boxes of it, unspent shells strewn across the third floor. Bullet cases thick as cockroaches. Hundreds of rounds sitting in closets, stashed in drawers, fanned across his mother's bed. The truth is, if the kid had had it in him, we might have been in a gun battle for days.

I was frankly stunned by the arsenal we uncovered; rifles and shotguns with enough ammo to supply a small army. All within easy grasp of a young man angry with his girlfriend and the world, dealing with significant personal problems, and apparently convinced violence could solve both.

Of course, there was more to this particular crime scene than weaponry, shell cases, and piles of physical evidence.

There was a human toll too, a tale of flesh and blood, suffering and death. The tale of cops on the other end of the fusillade. The men who took the worst of it, who felt the bullets pierce their flesh. And in one case, died.

So out of respect for those who suffered, and the one cop who gave his life, I'm going to commit their names to paper. The seven brave men who put themselves in harm's way. A memoriam for one; simple recognition for the others:

> Jimmy D. Holcombe, dead at the scene, age 31, a patrol officer from the Western District.
> Detective James A. Brennan, felled by two shotgun wounds to the arm and side.
> Officer Arthur Kendall, Western District, wounded by a shotgun blast to the arms and face.

Officer Calvin Menchen, Southern District, shotgun wound to the face.
Officer Neal Plain, Southern District, shotgun wounds to the face.
Officer Roland Miller, Western District, shot in the arm.
Officer George Weaver, Southern District, shot in the hands and face.

The final report was completed in 36 hours. More than 20 pages which described in painstaking detail each and every weapon, bullet casing, witness and injury. It was on the commissioner's desk signed and delivered before he could ask for it. Frankly I was exhausted, but I knew the worst was yet to come.

After it was finished, I think I slept for 24 hours straight. Not peaceful sleep, just sleep. Just waiting for the other shoe to drop.

THE AFTERMATH

Always, after a significant tragedy, there is both public and private hand-wringing. Redoubt and recrimination, and worst of all, finger pointing.

Media coverage of the Good Friday Massacre was in many ways similar to what occurs in the present. Stories about the psychological ills of the shooter, and his unfortunate access to weapons. Cautionary tales about mixing guns and mental illness. Questions about how we responded. If we were prepared. A lot of second-guessing.

Behind the scenes, tactical commanders voiced concerns as well. First, that crucial information was not relayed to them before the shooting occurred, and that their units weren't properly equipped. In a fairly lengthy analysis of the incident, they enumerated several lapses.

The street lights on Lombard Street should have been shot out sooner to provide better cover for officers. Smoke grenades should have been used to provide cover to clear wounded officers under fire. Gas canisters should have been shot into 1303 Lombard to disrupt Williams.

They also arrived at a fairly morbid conclusion: it could have been worse.

"I believe also that if the sniper was anyone but an 18-year-old," a commander wrote, "many other police and civilian personnel would have been killed or injured. Example: someone with a military background, who was a veteran of the Vietnam War with experience with jungle tactics and expertise in the use of weapons, would have been harder to apprehend and contain."

It was a sobering critique. Admitting we had done many things wrong, that we were not completely prepared, and in the end, not wholly organized... but also lucky. Very lucky.

Still, I'm not sure if anyone can be ready for a John Earl Williams. He, and others like him, have an overwhelming advantage: the element of surprise. They don't usually call us before they pick up a gun. And even when they do, like Williams, they're almost always not specific enough.

Truthfully, it's the mettle, bravery, and flexibility of the front-line troops that determine just how well you're going to respond.

In fact, if you look at the list of officers who were injured that day, you'll see what I mean. It was street cops who bore the brunt of the violence, not specialized tactical personnel or sharpshooters. Instead, patrol officers took the majority of the bullets. Those unheralded cops in the car and on foot who are usually first on the scene — and last to be recognized. Men who in 1976 were armed with a .38-caliber handgun and a nightstick.

Patrol is always front and center when the bullets start flying. In fact, they're really flex troops, people who know enough about anything and everything to respond to the unforeseen madman or unexpected catastrophe.

If I was asked today how to improve the city's police department and lower our national embarrassment of a homicide rate my answer would be simple: invest in patrol. But that's not exactly what happened.

In many ways, the shooting had some long-term implications for the BPD.

Certainly we beefed up our tactical units and adopted many of the recommendations made in the report about weaponry and tactics. And yes, we made changes in how we respond strategically to barricades, particularly when it comes to who brings gas canisters to the fight.

In fact, I think, the crazed-shooter phenomenon embodied by John Earl Williams contributed equally as much as terrorism towards militarizing police departments. It may be the type of crime that occurs only once every 40 years, but its repercussions can easily become institutionalized, creating an agency heavily invested in preparing for anomalous behavior, and less focused on commonplace crimes.

Tactics aside however, there was something I learned that day which still lives with me even now. Insight, if you could call it that, into human nature that has little to do with weaponry and tear gas. Something about the potential for bad behavior, and my concern that the notion we're powerless to stop it... could cause even thornier problems.

So now let's just work from the proposition that the carnage that Williams caused on the corner of Lombard and Carey Streets was completely preventable — yes, preventable. His actions were virtually predictable. And the eventual outcome, hardly improbable.

In the end, Williams could have been stopped — seriously, any of these shooters could be stopped — if we would only be willing give up a few things.

But first, a truism: People who pick up a gun and shoot anyone or everyone are a pretty small group. Let's say no more than a minute few in all the years that I've been a cop. But that doesn't mean there's a shortage of whackos who shoot a friend, a relative, or jilting lover. There are far too many in fact, who do.

But the truth is, spectacular crimes are as rare as they are horrific. If John Earl Williams had simply shot his girlfriend Joyce instead of seven cops, this wouldn't have been much of a story. So with that in mind, let's consider the remedy... and its consequences:

Begin by stationing armed cops on every corner of the city. Make it mandatory for all young men between the ages of 18-34 to report for bimonthly psychological counseling.

Ban all private ownership of handguns. Conduct random searches without a warrant. Tap the cellphones of each and every kid who has expressed an angry thought. Create checkpoints to frisk for guns.

Roll back the Constitution just a bit... just a bit. Put more cops on the streets. Add even more tactical units, and arm them with heavy duty weaponry. Beef up video surveillance, put a camera on every corner, and have someone watching it 24/7.

Fly drones over major cities.

And don't forget to pay for it. If necessary, we can increase taxes, cut school funding, and close parks to pay for it.

But we'll be safe, right? We won't have to worry about crazed killers, lone gunmen, radical terrorists and any other nut-jobs who pick up a gun. With added firepower for the police, we can rest assured that school shootings and mall murders will never happen again, correct?

Of course not!

As cops, we learn quickly there's an aspect of inevitability to human depravity. A certain number of people, for whatever reason, are going to behave badly no matter what we do. Maybe it's the price of real freedom, the freedom to screw up.

Call it the potential for anything to happen. Or the simple fact that sometimes, for no good reason, people do horrible things. It's hard to comprehend, and even harder to live with. But in the end, the best we can hope to do is mitigate the suffering when it happens.

Listen, if I thought banning assault weapons would prevent a madman from ever slaughtering innocent people for no good reason I'd advocate banning them posthaste. Finally and forever.

But it would never work, because the real problem would still be around — us.

I understand that the assault rifle affords a murderer a whole lot more potential to kill. I get it that being able to fire off a hundred rounds a minute can turn a deadly shooter into a mass murderer. I acknowledge there is no good reason for a deer hunter to own an AR-15 magazine-fed semi-automatic rifle or to need any other assault rifle for that matter.

But I think passing a law, clamping down on freedom, and creating another huge government bureaucracy to administer it is a treacherous compromise. Because freedom is a responsibility, our responsibility, not the government's. The more we hand it over, the less it belongs to us. Just look at the war on drugs and its cost: billions of dollars, prisons everywhere, and even worse, a weakened Bill of Rights.

Truth be told, I don't think even Williams' rampage was inevitable. We did some checking into his background. Turns out he was discharged from the military. He had stolen a gun once with some friends shortly before the shootout with us. He needed help, not from cops, but from the community.

If you really want to prevent violence, take Williams' case as an example. Think beyond policing and towards more productive outcomes, something other than prison. Maybe we should put more money and resources into keeping young men busy. Give them something to do, distract them, or better yet, make them useful.

As I stated in the first chapter of this book, I was a troublemaker as a kid, like Williams. I had problems with authority. I liked to take risks and cause trouble. I didn't stay in school; I didn't have plans for the future. I was, to put it simply, a loser.

But luckily I found something to do, a purpose. The minute I put on a uniform something changed. In policing, I discovered something I was good at, something through which I could contribute.

As a society we're quick to build prisons, and fill them. We have no problem expanding police budgets, finding money for overtime when after-school programs are simultaneously being cut. It's all because the honest answers don't jibe with the simplicity of politics.

Cracking down, getting tough, throwing the book, accomplish one politically expedient goal: taking the onus off the rest of us. Casting the responsibility for the radical others onto cops, judges, and jailers.

Forget self reflection and personal responsibility. Forget the hard work of building a community. Somebody was responsible for Williams.

Someone in the community knew he was troubled; someone should have stepped up and taken an interest. A parent, a friend, a guardian, or even a cop on the beat in his neighborhood should have intervened.

But that's too hard, too complex, and too sticky. You can't simply pass a law or give a speech, you have to think.

But like I've already stated, there's always a certain number of people who will behave badly no matter what. A percentage of human beings who will commit crimes regardless of how many walls you build. There simply seems to be as much potential for destructive behavior as there is productive. As if people are simply born to test the boundaries of the former.

The truth is — the truth no one wants to hear — is that you can't stop them all... and even if you could, the price you'd pay wouldn't be worth it.

But maybe the extreme cases are supposed to teach us something. Maybe Williams' rampage reminds us about an aspect of human nature we'd like to forget. His crime reveals what we lack, what we don't have. The void of contemporary life.

How numbers and stats and surveillance and catastrophic weapons and SWAT teams have replaced the single cop on the beat, with little thought given to the consequences for a human community. How the impulses that course through our veins urge contradictory choices: the freedom to be good and freedom to be bad. How young men today are often wedded to the screen, of films and violent computer games, with little sense of themselves beyond the realm of fantasy.

Williams' anger could be a confirmation and yet a condemnation of all this. Of the world we've built, an infrequent and unfortunate reminder of how we need to do better. Not only at being cops, but as people who naturally take responsibility for their own behavior.

CHAPTER THREE:
WHAT IS A CRIME?

The Shooting at City Hall

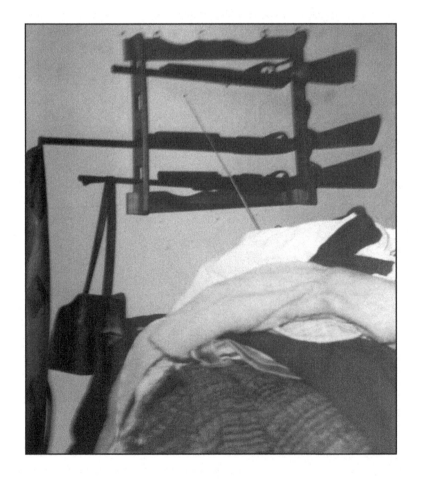

What is *crime*?

What I'm asking is, what do we mean when we use the word?

I know it sounds like a stupid question, especially for a cop. Show me an officer who doesn't think he understands it. Who doesn't reflexively conjure up breaking the law, bad behavior, and destructive activities like drug dealing when the word comes to mind.

It's simple, right? Or is it?

Since it was my job as a detective to solve crimes, I've thought quite a bit about what the word really means. But not because I don't understand it, per se. That's not the point.

But as a cop who enforces the law, I find the word to be misleading, overly simple. In fact, I'm not sure if the word matches the problem it purports to define.

What do I mean? Put simply, the word crime conjures up many types of human behavior that don't always reconcile into a neat category.

And therein lies the dilemma.

Think about it, a junky gets a bag of raw, ducks into an empty row home and shoots up. Is that a crime? Similarly, a neighborhood kid from a broken home starts stealing lawn mowers for no particular reason; is that a crime? A woman shoots her abusive husband in the leg after a severe beating; is that a crime?

According to the aforementioned definition, all those acts of human stupidity are classified as crimes. Crimes that are added up, booked as a stat, and more often than not, end with someone spending time in jail.

But is that what we really mean when we invoke the word? And if we're trying to reduce crime, so to speak, does that very definition point us in the right direction to solve the problems which define it?

That's why I'm asking the question, What is crime?

And what does it really mean when the crime rate is up?... which is supposedly a bad portent. Or when crime is down?... which, conversely, is "good."

What do crime stats tell us about the health of the community we live in? Crime on the rise, we put more police on the street. Crime on the decline, decreasing, we give cops the credit. It's simple, right?

Well maybe not. Maybe that's too neat, too compact, like a creed or religion we all accept without question because it's simply easier than reexamining what it means.

But maybe it's time we started questioning it.

By sweeping all this dysfunction into a single concept, do we really understand what we're talking about? Have we used the word without thinking about the complex problems that underlie it?

If you think I'm off my rocker, take a drive around Baltimore City, particularly the East or West Side.

Better yet, head over to North Broadway and drive east below Johns Hopkins Hospital. You'll find whole blocks lined with nothing but abandoned row homes. Not a single person, family, dog, cop, kid... not a single sign of life. Not a car or a barbeque or a note of music to be heard. Nor a baby crying, a meal cooking, or a game being played by children on the street.

Nothing, just a land of vacants.

And that's because of crime, right?

That's what we were told: we had to make our communities safe. If they're unsafe, we're not whole, right? That was the mantra, safety first. Bring in the cops. Hire more police.

And we did.

Fight crime. And we did.

Lower the crime rate... and supposedly we have.

And yet, now we have an entirely different problem.

Emptiness.

We attacked crime and won silence. We fought for safety and gained brick-layered graves of desolate row homes. We criminalized neighborhoods with thousands of unnecessary and often illegal arrests.

Which is why I'm troubled by the generalizations that stem from using the word.

Crime.

Maybe the aforementioned junky needs drug treatment and the wayward teen a mentor. Maybe the beleaguered neighborhood needs investment and self rule.

But if we deem certain acts as crimes without examining the myriad factors which precipitate them, then it's up to the cops and courts to solve the problem. And that means arrests, jails, and lots of money, and the resulting emptiness that pervades large swaths of the city.

Still, whether you agree me with me or not, our thinking about the word and the chaos it represents, will be hard to change. It's a theology ingrained in the public consciousness, and most of all, in the heads of our so-called leaders. Crime is an effective rhetorical tool for engendering fear, compliance, and electoral consent. It's a malleable catchphrase that turns overly simple solutions into compelling campaign narratives.

And in Baltimore, it's a word that inevitably pushed the city into a war with itself. An ongoing battle between cops and communities that one could argue is as destructive as the underlying behavior it was implemented to stop.

I remember a tragic day when the conflicting meanings of the word collided. When violence erupted from the fissures of an untreated mental illness. And when the tendrils of social dysfunction that were spreading onto the streets of Baltimore finally touched the upper echelons of the city's elite.

A crime so unexpected it changed the character of a community forever, and did more to solidify our philosophy of crime into the ongoing referendum to control dysfunctional behavior with ever more punitive techniques.

The day a man committed murder inside Baltimore City Hall.

OPEN FOR TROUBLE

It's hard to imagine. But in 1976, the City Hall of one of the largest communities in the country did not have security. No cops; no metal detectors; no closed-circuit cameras stationed at the entrance. No weapons or locked doors or areas designated off-limits.

No, the entirety of security inside the headquarters of what was then the tenth largest city in the country consisted of a receptionist sitting at a desk inside the door of the then-temporary City Hall on Guilford Avenue, and what was known as a "watchman," a security guard in name only, who roamed the halls, mostly in the evenings.

With just a uniform and a flashlight.

So I can only assume that on the day a man named Charles Anthony Hopkins showed up to badger city officials about difficulties he was having getting permits for his business, no one took much notice. In fact, the truth is, despite his reported odd behavior and awkward hostility, people literally tried to help him.

Hopkins was a young African-American who had recently purchased a restaurant on North Avenue. But the eatery was equipped with an aging fryer that prompted the city Health Department to close it down.

And now the business was in legal limbo because Hopkins couldn't afford to replace the faulty fryer. Without a new fryer he couldn't get the permits he needed to re-open. In the meantime, his landlord was dunning him for rent and an inspector in the food bureau wasn't returning his calls.

Bottom line, his dream was starting to slip away.

So on April 12, 1976 Hopkins simply walked into the temporary City Hall Headquarters on Guilford Avenue, holding a brown paper bag. The sweaty, wily young man wearing maroon pants and leisure jacket — stylish for that period — placed the bag on the receptionist's desk and asked to speak with then-Mayor William Donald Schaefer.

Or, I should say, demanded.

That's because the receptionist later recalled that Hopkins became "agitated" when the mayor didn't immediately appear. In fact, she recalled summoning an aide from the mayor's office to stand watch at her desk.

Put simply, Hopkins made her nervous.

Of course, plenty of people at City Hall that day would later describe Hopkins' behavior as erratic and odd. First there was the aforementioned paper bag with mysterious contents that Hopkins kept under wraps. Then his offhand threatening remarks to bystanders which punctuated his encounters throughout the day.

"Why aren't you doing your job?" he barked at a Schaefer aide.

"Who's responsible for this mess?" he yelled at another staffer.

Still, he continued to press the receptionist for a meeting with the mayor. Finally fed up, she summoned a Schaefer aide. The aide politely asked Hopkins how he could help him.

Hopkins said he was having trouble with his business and wanted a meeting with Schaefer to discuss it. The aide told Hopkins the mayor didn't get involved in disputes involving businesses.

And that's when he snapped. The first sign he wasn't your average disgruntled business owner.

"The only thing people at City Hall will truly understand is violence," he threatened.

"Call the police and have me removed," he yelled, then screamed a final insult as he stormed out the door:

"You're a bunch of Uncle Tom niggers and hillbilly bitches!"

Inexplicably, he returned later to City Hall. We're not sure how or when, but he made his way onto the ninth floor where he burst into a meeting of the Board of Estimates, the body which approves city contracts and procurements. To the astonishment of former Comptroller Hyman Pressman and City Councilwoman Mary Pat Clarke, Hopkins started grilling the assembled city leaders, wielding his paper bag like a cudgel.

"What are you all getting paid for?" he asked the stunned group as he reiterated his demand to meet with Schaefer.

Clarke quickly jumped to her feet and escorted Hopkins to a nearby conference room.

That's when Hopkins launched into a diatribe about his ailing business. Rent he owed to a landlord who didn't adequately maintain the building. An intransigent city Health Department which had closed down the shop three weeks before it was due to open because he didn't have the right equipment. An inspector from the Bureau of Food Control who wouldn't return his calls. In short, a litany of ills exacerbated by a dwindling bank account, that quickly descended into a rant about rats, roaches, and other pests.

Clarke told Hopkins she would try to help, but that she couldn't solve his problems "in a day." He replied that he was part of an activist group known as "The Shack" and asked the councilwoman if she would meet with them. She agreed, so Hopkins boarded an elevator and appeared to leave the building.

However there were other sightings that day of Hopkins. Several City Council members recalled spotting him watching a birthday party for a council staff member, accompanied by a white woman and a white male. Another staffer saw him wandering the seventh floor near the mayor's office.

Many staffers simply recalled random outbursts. Threats that he would return and "change the way things are done around here," or promises to use violence to "get his way." But the truth is, disgruntled business owners and citizens with an ax to grind were common around City Hall. So even though Hopkins made an impression, no one bothered to report it to the police.

So the very next day, Tuesday, April 13, 1976, when he returned, Hopkins didn't have to waste time asking questions. In fact, he was so obviously agitated the receptionist called the same aide out of her office, asking her in a hushed voice to hang around.

Hopkins again badgered the aide. He asked her again to explain to him why he couldn't see the mayor. And again, the staffers tried to persuade him to seek help elsewhere. The mayor, they told him, didn't get involved in contract disputes.

But Hopkins stormed past the receptionist, boarded an elevator and made his way to the seventh floor toward the office of the mayor.

It's tragic, in retrospect, that we didn't have just one cop working City Hall that day. Honestly, looking back it's hard to believe that no one had thought of increasing security inside the building, especially in light of what had happened the day before.

I mean, the streets in the 1970s were awash in blood; we were booking 300 murders a year. And yet, the lack of City Hall security shows in part that violent crime had yet to scathe the city's elite in a direct way. Even after the riots of 1968 when the entire West and East Sides of Baltimore were set aflame following the assassination of Martin Luther King in Tennessee, the central headquarters of Baltimore City government didn't even have a security guard armed with a walkie-talkie, let alone a gun.

So when Hopkins proceeded to the seventh floor of City Hall with his sights set on the mayor, the only people between him and his target were female aides. Typists, a receptionist and desk workers "armed" with ballpoint pens. A psychopath hell-bent on killing the city's chief executive whose only obstacle was an office staff of women. An irrational, irate man armed with a gun marching towards a secretary pool.

And indeed the first person he encountered was the mayor's appointments secretary, Charlotte Bethke. She told us he followed her into the office of Kathleen Nolan, a typist. As she watched in horror, Hopkins pulled a black gun from his pocket as Nolan asked who he was and what he wanted.

"I'll tell you who I am," he barked, aiming the gun at her head.

"Put that gun away," Nolan ordered, defiantly.

And that's when it happened, the first shot. Frustrated, angry, and off-kilter — who knows? — Hopkins fired a single bullet at Nolan, hitting her in the chest.

"Oh God, I've been shot!" she cried, a gaping bullet wound in her left side.

Hopkins exited the office back into the hallway. There he came face to face with a mayoral aide named Linda Fasteau.

It was a terrifying rendezvous, Fasteau recalled. Hopkins just stared at her, gun at his side still smoking from the discharge. Sweat gleaming from his brow and Nolan's cries filling the hallway. And now he was simply standing in the hallway looking confused.

Just then another aide named Joanne McQuade rushed into the hallway. She also recalled hearing a gunshot, and then running toward Nolan's office. When she arrived Nolan was clutching her left breast.

"He shot me," Nolan cried out.

McQuade sprinted to the front desk to use the receptionist's phone to call for help. But as she lifted the receiver, she turned to see Hopkins pointing his gun directly at her.

"Hang up the phone or I'll shoot you," Hopkins ordered.

"Where's the mayor?" he then demanded, the gun now pointed at her head.

"He's in Annapolis," she replied.

Indeed Schaefer *was* in Annapolis. Hopkins' intended target was long gone.

Seemingly unfazed by the news, Hopkins walked calmly towards her and grabbed her by the collar. He then spun her around placing the gun at the back of her head.

"I'm going down to the city councilmen's office," he barked. "You better take me to the right office or I'll blow your head off."

What happened next is hard to explain. That's because McQuade acted like a well-trained cop, not an officer worker.

One of the most beguiling aspects of significant tragedies is how often ordinary people behave in extraordinary ways. When I say ordinary people, I mean people who aren't trained for tragedy. Citizens without guns or badges, just courage. In fact, it seems tragic events often surprisingly spawn unlikely heroes.

Consider the passengers on United Airlines Flight 93 on September 11, 2001. Rugby players and tech salesmen banding together to stop terrorists who had eluded authorities. Untrained yet incredibly resourceful and heroic Americans accomplishing what the entirety of U.S. law enforcement could not do.

We all know the story. How they stormed the cockpit with little hope of survival. How they sacrificed their lives for the greater good. How they took down a plane that was likely headed toward the Capitol or the White House. How they died to prevent a disaster of even more ominous consequences.

And just like the heroes of that infamous flight, what Joanne McQuade did next still confounds me. A person who was typing a memo minutes before, she was unexpectedly thrust into a fight for her life. A City Hall staffer accustomed to council meetings and dictation now feeling the cold barrel of a gun on the back of her neck.

And what did she do? How did she handle this unexpected brush with death?

She tried to de-escalate it. Better still, she attempted to confuse her assailant.

"Are you sure you don't want me to get you out of the building so you can get away?" she asked.

Wow!

Still, Hopkins didn't bite. Instead he forced her toward a bank of elevators. Finally convinced the mayor was nowhere to be found, he told her he wanted to speak to someone on the council.

"Do what I just told you," he ordered. "Take me to the councilmen's office."

When the elevator didn't arrive quickly enough, Hopkins dragged her down the stairs and onto the sixth floor, the home of council members' offices.

At the temporary City Hall Headquarters, council quarters were clustered along a hallway. Inner sanctums, punctuated with secretary stations.

Hopkins arrived with McQuade in tow. He jumped a gate at the entrance and for reasons still unknown headed towards the office of Councilman Dominic Leone.

Councilman Leone was a larger than life character peculiar to Baltimore. Large, in the physical sense, with an equally outsized personality. The esteemed *Baltimore Sun* columnist and former *News American* reporter Michael Olesker described the councilman as "great fun. In slow moments, you could find the senior Leone on the floor of his council office, sleeves rolled up, a Marlboro dangling from his lips and dice in his hand."

I didn't know the councilman, but I'd heard Olesker's characterization of the man rang true.

That fateful day, an election worker named William Berkman was in Leone's office when Hopkins barged through an open door.

"Who are you?" Hopkins asked Berkman.

"I'm nobody," Berkman replied.

Leone got up from his desk, raising his hands.

"Now wait a minute, fellow," was all the councilman was able to utter before Hopkins fired. A quick shot, Berkman recalled, "without warning or provocation."

Berkman bolted from the office as another shot rang out, the sound of gunfire scattering staffers and council members who scrambled for impromptu cover or barricaded themselves behind closed doors.

Unbeknownst to them, Hopkins had claimed his first life. In an instant, a councilman, a city leader, a family man and father, a part of Baltimore's cast of legendary flamboyance, was dead before he hit the floor.

Still, Hopkins wasn't finished.

Witnesses say he stormed from Leone's office and started shooting indiscriminately. First at a man running down the hall, then another shot fired in the direction of Councilman Carroll J. Fitzgerald, who was standing outside the office of Councilman Joseph Curran Sr.

Hopkins missed again.

Curran was able to duck back inside his office where he lay upon the floor and put his feet against the door.

But Hopkins forced his way into Fitzgerald's office. An aide researching the city's curfew law recalled that Hopkins stormed into the office, pointed his gun at him, and ordered Fitzgerald and the aide to both sit down.

"Are you the mayor," Hopkins asked. "I need to speak to the mayor."

Wild-eyed and sweaty, Hopkins grabbed the stunned Fitzgerald by the neck and pointed the weapon at the councilman's head. Then, still apparently delusional, he dragged the councilman down the sixth-floor corridor screaming at bystanders and gesticulating wildly.

With Fitzgerald in tow, Hopkins mounted the stairwell back towards the seventh floor.

"Take me to the mayor," he demanded.

A city employee named Frank Wiggington encountered the pair as they stumbled into the hallway.

"Stay back, stay back," Fitzgerald warned.

Several other employees who were gathered by the elevator watched in horror. The stunned onlookers gaped as Hopkins dragged Fitzgerald by the collar as he ordered them to board the elevator.

By now, calls were streaming into Police Headquarters. Frantic 911 callers reporting shots fired, colleagues injured, and an active shooter on the loose.

About a half-dozen officers responded to the seventh floor. But it was too late.

Remember what I said about ordinary people who do extraordinary things in extreme situations? The heroic behavior I've witnessed on more than one occasion where a civilian simply confounded expectations. Well you can count Councilman Fitzgerald as another example. A civilian who decided he wasn't going to go down without a fight. A councilman determined not to suffer the same fate as his colleague.

When officers arrived on the seventh floor, they spotted Hopkins in an erratic retreat. The panicky gunman dragging Fitzgerald by the collar in a serpentine withdrawal, his crazed hunt for the mayor dissembling into a blind and unhinged effort to survive.

The chase quickly turned into a game of cat and mouse. Hopkins ducking in-between cubicles. Cops trying to get a clean shot at him. But as they closed in... gunfire.

"I've been shot!" Fitzgerald yelled.

Rushing into a maze of back-office cubicles they came upon a scene of mortal struggle: Hopkins and Fitzgerald in a twisted embrace fighting for the gun. The councilman wounded. Hopkins bent backwards like a gymnast, still struggling to keep his grip on the pistol.

The officers pounced on Hopkins, who managed to momentarily break free. They opened fire, striking him several times.

And that quickly it was over, at least in part. Hopkins was subdued, City Hall was locked down. For the moment, at least, there was peace. An end to mayhem — brought about largely by civilians like Councilman Fitzgerald.

Still, Fitzgerald paid a price for his bravery: he suffered a gunshot wound to the abdomen. Kathy Nolan too, was shot in the left side and required surgery. One of the responding officers was shot in the leg.

Hopkins suffered six gunshot wounds, four shots in the left and right sides of his stomach, a shot through his left arm and a bullet wound that grazed his pinkie.

Sadly, councilman Leone was pronounced dead at the scene, an unlucky victim of a deranged shooter with an indiscriminate beef.

Kathy Nolan, who was shot through the left side, recovered. So too did Councilman Fitzgerald. In hindsight, we were lucky.

But there was another casualty, a mortal wound inflicted that day which would turn fatal nearly a year later.

Councilman Joe Curran, father of former state Attorney General Joseph Curran Jr. and current Councilman Robert Curran, suffered a heart attack shortly after the rampage. It was a serious, nearly deadly event for him. He didn't die that day, but he never fully recovered.

A year later, his heart gave out. A fatal heart attack caused by a shot fired a year before his death. To this day, his family blames the councilman's demise on Hopkins, and rightly so.

Of course, unlike his victims, Hopkins managed to survive multiple gunshot wounds.

During the rampage a total of five shots were fired by three police officers. Hopkins himself fired four well-aimed shots plus others, three that hit their mark: The mortal wound to Councilman Leone, the bullet in the side of Kathleen Nolan; the shot at Councilman Curran, and the shot to the abdomen that wounded Councilman Fitzgerald.

One person dead, another a year later. Two others wounded, with just four bullets.

Shortly after the shooting we executed a search warrant at Hopkins' home at 1240 North Curley Street. We wanted to obtain samples of his handwriting to compare his penmanship to a note received by the Chesapeake & Potomac Telephone Company. It was an incoherent, rambling diatribe against the mayor, an anonymous threat to commit violence, grammatically challenged but nevertheless chilling:

"Now we are going to sometimes like they do on the other side and start bombing building down and all so we are going to get that bum Mayor house or car up while he is in or kidnap him so we hope youre the big shots of the telephone co will understand this to the big shots."

We turned the letter over to a criminologist for analysis, who concluded that Hopkins probably wrote it. A small piece of the puzzle uncovered after the fact, yet little consolation to the dead. But an affirmation of my long-held belief as a cop: there are always warning signs.

In fact, looking back, the shooting at City Hall was a warning to the city itself. The frustration and inability of one man to deal with the reality of his own failures foisted upon the entire staff of City Hall in the form of indiscriminate violence. An emblematic confrontation between his slow descent into dysfunction and our political inability to prevent it.

It's hard today to understand, I think, how quickly the city was changing then. We were in the throes of the most violent decade of the twentieth century. As I said before, the homicide floor at Police Headquarters was inundated with 300 killings per year. In 1968 the entire city was engulfed in riots after the death of Dr. Martin Luther King Jr. There was the vigilante group called Black October picking off drug dealers and bragging about it. All told, violence erupted just as the city's fiscal fortunes began a long and ugly decline.

In a sense, the city was turning inward upon itself.

I think the shooting at City Hall was a watershed moment. The genteel air of a familial City Hall had been shattered by the harsh reality of indiscriminate violence. The often incomprehensible bloodshed occurring on the streets of the city's poorest neighborhoods found its way into a world unaccustomed to it.

I'm not saying that city leaders weren't troubled by the city's body count, or that the political class wasn't struggling to find a way to stop it. People cared then, and they care now. In fact, every person Hopkins encountered as he stalked City Hall, tried to help. They were polite to a fault.

What I'm trying to say is the fact that a man frustrated with his lot in life would use a gun to achieve redress was simply a new and frightening type of crime for all of us.

Looking back I think outbursts like Hopkins' were a warning sign, a symptom of a communal sepsis just starting to take hold. An inauspicious trend that portended the decades of death to come.

And that's why I started out this chapter meditating on the word crime. Because it turns out Hopkins' murderous rampage wasn't a crime at all, at least according to our definition. A Baltimore City judge found him not criminally responsible for the death of Councilman Dominic Leone and the attempted murder of Councilman Fitzgerald and Kathy Dolan. He was declared insane and remanded for treatment to a state mental hospital.

Nearly 30 years later from the day he stormed into City Hall wielding a gun, Hopkins walked free. A state board determined he was in fact now sane, no longer a threat to society. Just a regular citizen who had picked up a gun and killed a man. And terrorized a city government.

It's an outcome that begs the question I raised at the beginning of this chapter:

If Hopkins' decision to storm City Hall, brandish a gun, and shoot innocent people isn't a crime, then what is? Was he really too crazy to understand that gunning down innocent people was wrong? Was his mind so beset with demons that he was incapable of finding another way to resolve his gripes?

If it was insanity, then was it the type of craziness born of an inability to deal with the frustration and consequences of bad choices? a failure to grasp that the flipside of free will is the unpalatable freedom to fail?

Or could it be a more insidious indictment of the city's character then, and now?

A city that was once one of the wealthiest in the nation at a loss on how to rectify its failing economic fortunes? A city so used to fighting over the spoils of industrialization that it could not reconfigure itself to re-deploy hundreds of thousands of people thrown out of work?

Maybe we were just starting to feel the pushback from years of entrenched corruption. A stranglehold on progress that elicited rebuke in the form of bullets.

What I do know is that Hopkins' horrible crimes that day spurred changes at City Hall. Today when you visit you'll be frisked by cops and forced to walk through a metal detector. There are never fewer than two police officers stationed at the front entrance at all times. And unless there's a public hearing or a council meeting, you can't just roam around the building without an approved destination or a person that you're authorized to see.

And it also I think started the slow sea change in the thinking about crime that might have sent us down a very treacherous path: the idea that the aforementioned string of violence was a wave of crime in and of itself. In other words, we were unsafe, because the city was engulfed in crime. Bad behavior that could be corrected or even prevented with force.

How could you blame us? A man had just carried a gun into City Hall and shot people he didn't even know. What kind of person does such a thing? And what kind of city produces 300 killers a year, not to mention an 18-year-old sniper who guns down seven cops?

It's the type of social unrest that causes panic and fear, and with it, searches for immediate solutions, quick fixes, a bandage on the wound, so to speak. When people start shooting, we also stop thinking. It's just human; understandable and predictable.

But I wonder if we didn't miss the forest for the trees? If the import and consequences we imbued to the word crime didn't mislead us?

Think about it, all these murders, killings and violence, why was it happening now? The bottomless sense of antipathy toward fellow human beings, what were the core causes? And isn't it interesting, just as the city's industrial base truly began to destabilize, that the population's thirst for violence began its long unholy ascent? Is it just coincidence that as our economic infrastructure started to fray, our sense of humanity began to dissemble with it?

I think not. In fact, that's why I lament the word crime. The categorization of behavior it engenders. The generalizations about behavior it elicits. I think had we taken a more nuanced look at what was happening back then, we might have been able to prevent some of the bloodiest decades in the history of any city. We might have diagnosed the broader sense of social disorder our impending fiscal collapse was brewing in broken homes and unrealized dreams.

We might have perceived our battle against crime as a war against ourselves. That unleashing enforcement to tackle a social illness was cutting off our communal nose, to spite our civic face.

Because that's what the war on crime, drugs and other maladies became in some sense — a deadly game of spite. An ongoing escalation of physical force and firepower that builds prisons and puts more cops on the street without considering the destructive consequences of both. It set us on the path of confronting despair and dysfunction with enforcement. And if you think it worked, as I said before, drive around.

Take a look at the city and what our definition of the word crime has wrought. Take a minute to consider what fear begets when we succumb to it. It's easy to see, and even easier to understand.

As scared as we are, and as necessary as fighting random violence from terrorist attacks by rampage shooters can be, there's always something lost when we make the decision to fight back by increasing the power of any bureaucracy, including the police department. A political price we pay when we go to war with ourselves can be measured in the thousands of lives lost, disrupted, and held captive by the burgeoning business of justice.

But I'm not inveighing against policing. Not at all. There are plenty of people who belong in jail. Irremediable criminals who should be behind bars so that the community can live in peace.

The case of the City Hall shooting is illustrative of my point. It's the best example of my cautionary tale about policing. Because when Hopkins decided to wield a gun inside the corridors of city government, it was the community, not the cops, who stood defiantly in his way. It was average citizens, not armed guards, who stopped him. It was courageous women who put obstacles in his path, not burly men wielding guns.

It's a phenomenon that is supported by research. A recent analysis of 16 rampage shootings found that in 13 cases the gunman was disarmed by civilians before police could arrive. That means nearly 80 percent of the time the community was not only the first line of defense, but the most effective counteragent to a madman.

That's the funny thing about crime, the extreme behavior it elicits, and the lessons we can learn from that. It's such a complex process. An act precipitated by a series of circumstances that aren't always inevitable. A sequence of events often defined by one spectacular moment. A pattern of behavior that seems almost inevitable after the fact.

But is it?

Think about it: Could a call from a health inspector, a break on the rent from his landlord, or even a better sense of business acumen have derailed Hopkins from his murderous rampage and rendezvous with fate? Could a more vibrant economy, a growing sense of opportunity have kept him from pulling the trigger?

Could even a minor brush with a cop in the corridors of City Hall have defused the murderous moment forever?

These are questions that may seem irrelevant now, but are in fact the key to understanding crime as a barometer of social disorder if your goal is to stop it. Questions that always played out in my mind when I was tasked with investigating a tragedy that couldn't be undone. Doubts that lingered every time I stepped onto a crime scene.

Which is why, late in my life and at the end of my police career, I'm asking all of us to reconsider it. To think about crime not just as an event, or a bad act, but as a culmination of choices. Bad choices by the offender, and perhaps misguided strategies by the body politic.

It's the type of examination that needs to occur. A new way of thinking perhaps.

Or maybe just the last request of an old man.

In either case, if reconsideration can save even just one life, isn't it worth the effort?

CHAPTER FOUR:
A SICKNESS UNTO DEATH

My Encounter with a Sociopath

I have stood on the field of death and seen the truth.

Mortality is a bitch. It leaves us to rot like husks in the grass, to stink of decay till we wither away to nothing.

To stumble upon a corpse, to see the human form in all its ill-conceived temporality, is to be forever changed.

The body is a capricious instrument. Fragile and quickly dissembled once we vacate it. A mass of discoloration and nauseating pigments consumed in a process that is as unsettling as it is natural.

But surprisingly, the finality and the ignominy of death do little to curb the human thirst for inflicting it, especially in the City of Baltimore.

During my career as a homicide lieutenant, we notched no fewer than 300 killings each and every year, as I reiterate throughout this book. It's a number that gives me pause, even to this day. Not just the quantity of murders, but the collective act of malice the figure represents.

Remember, killing requires killers. That is, murders happen because people make bad choices.

Almost every day someone in Baltimore decides to murder. Without exception, at some point during a typical afternoon or evening, a prospective killer picks up a gun, brandishes a knife or some other weapon with intent to kill.

Thus it is the apparent stubbornness of our murderous impulse which defines us. We behave like a diseased communal mind in a perpetual premeditative state. The city's clockwork-like penchant for killing became the strangest and most unsettling aspect of my job.

Daily I would arrive on the Homicide floor, sit down at my desk, and wait for someone to die. I knew, sooner rather than later, somewhere someone was going to decide to take a life. The very fact that I and 30-some-odd detectives had a full-time job meant that the city's capacity for homicide was as predictable as the Sparrows Point steel assembly line.

Eventually, be it an hour or a day, but rarely more, the phone on the Homicide floor would ring with a report of a lifeless body in a ditch, in a gutter, tossed in an alley or laid out in a vacant lot. No matter how hard we tried to stop it, murder marched onward in Baltimore, as inevitable as it was destructive.

I was often surprised how little impetus it took to motivate someone to take a life. As I have already memorialized in this book, City Hall shooter Charles Anthony Hopkins was dead-set on killing the mayor because he couldn't get a permit for his restaurant. A permit! Or what about the kid who shot seven cops because his girlfriend dumped him?

I remember discussing Baltimore's propensity for killing with an unrepentant drug dealer. Not a philosophical discussion per se, but a simple query into his motivation.

He'd just killed a guy who owed him $500, a hapless street-level pusher who gave too much product away. The young man couldn't pay his weekly tab, and as a result was shot in the head in an alley off Biddle Street. The dealer was nonplussed. The murder charges, he believed, beatable. The killing, thoroughly justified.

Needless to say, the victim never paid up. So I asked the dealer if he'd ever considered the probability that killing the debtor would make collecting unlikely, even impossible?

"How were you going to get the cash after he was dead?" I asked.

"I didn't care," he replied without blinking an eye. "At least I had the satisfaction of killing him."

It was his story and other cases which reveal that the threshold for pulling the trigger in Baltimore was, and apparently still is, pretty low. The consequence of that particular impulsivity, I witnessed every day. Thousands of decisions to kill that resulted in the thick pile of file folders sitting on my desk.

But I didn't truly understand this impulse, the desire, or unstoppable will to take a life — until it was directed at me. That is, only when I was in the crosshairs did I gain true insight into this world of murder. It was when I was the target of Baltimore's unfathomable malice that I learned some remarkable truths about killing.

It may seem callous, or even self-serving, but to understand the plight of the victim, to truly comprehend the monstrous fear of the intended target, I had to experience it firsthand.

It was a case which included a maniacal union boss, some wildcat strikers, a couple of go-go dancers, and a sociopath. A cast of characters mixed up in a plan to use violence for uncertain ends, that disintegrated into a threat against *me*.

And it all started with a body left in a ditch, wrapped in a blanket, found by the Baltimore County Police on August 26th 1965.

BAD ACTORS

The victim, a man named Phillip Fiorino, was dumped off the side of Chesaco Avenue just north of Pulaski Highway. He'd been shot multiple times, twice in the head and once in the back.

Initially, he was just another corpse in a bloodthirsty town. As I noted earlier, we were bagging 300-plus bodies a year. And this guy had a pretty serious rap sheet: assaults, gun charges, and an attempted murder case he'd beaten a year earlier. Bottom line, it was hardly a surprise that Fiorino ended up stone cold dead on the side of the road.

But of course, this is Baltimore, and a homicide detective learns pretty quickly: Murders occur in bunches. Violence doesn't happen in a vacuum.

Investigating a murder is like telling a story backwards. The evidence of the present only makes sense when fitted to the facts of the past. And that's where this tale actually began.

At the time Fiorino's body was found, I was a sergeant working my first murder case. Not because anyone wanted me investigating homicides; in fact, there was more than a little pushback when I told my lieutenant I had a source with information that might tie Fiorino's murder to a high profile killing.

The murder of Kenneth Hatfield.

Hatfield was a shop steward/business agent for the Bricklayers Union. He'd been managing workers on the site of a new medical facility under construction on the Johns Hopkins Hospital campus. But the work was abruptly halted by a wildcat strike called by a notorious union boss, Guido Iozzi.

Iozzi was the president of the Baltimore Building Trades Council in the 1960s. Unlike Hatfield, he was feared, and ruled with an iron fist. My source told me it was Iozzi's idea to strike against the hospital. A bid by a powerful union boss to increase wages against one of the wealthiest institutions in town by bringing work on a critical addition to the hospital campus to a complete halt.

Hatfield didn't support the strike. From what I was told he thought it was too risky, a ploy that might endanger jobs. So the union leader made a fateful decision: He told his men to cross the picket line.

It was a decision that likely led to a knock on his front door on the evening of August 20th 1965.

"Are you Ken Hatfield?" asked a man standing on the porch.

"Yes," he replied.

Without warning the unseen inquisitor shoved a .22-caliber pistol against the screen door and fired two shots. Hatfield fell to the floor critically wounded — but the gunman wasn't finished. As the 43-year-old bricklayer writhed on the floor of his home, the murderer fired off two more rounds, this time in the back, killing him instantly.

From the beginning Hatfield's murder smelled like a mob hit. The victim was as clean as a whistle. He was a respected union leader well-liked by his co-workers.

So who were his enemies? Who wanted him dead? Was his decision to defy the union a deadly mistake?

Of course, Baltimore still had remnants of its industrial might, and labor unions then were a force to be reckoned with. Remember, the city was home to a million people, a General Motors Plant on Broening Highway, and the still mighty Sparrows Point steel mill and shipyard. Unions had power and union leaders were not afraid to wield it.

But all this was unknown to me until I got a tip from an informant. A tip that would lead me on a collision course with one of the most ruthless men I'd ever met.

The informant told me Hatfield's murder was a botched job, and that the man who screwed it up was the same person we found lying in the ditch: Phillip Fiorino.

The tipster said Fiorino was only supposed to frighten Hatfield, rough him up a little. Scare him into honoring the picket line. But the trigger-happy gunman had blown it, literally. The result: a dead union leader and pissed-off union boss. The word was, Fiorino's mistake cost him his life.

So the informant suggested I talk to the occupants of an apartment at 19 West Preston Street. According to him, that's where the trail of death began, and ended.

And so I did, and what I uncovered was not only an epic mess, but as I said before, led me to a sociopath whose disregard for life still haunts me to this day.

A STRIPPER, A MAN NAMED IRISH, AND A BODY

We started the investigation by bringing the occupants of the apartment at 19 West Preston down to Homicide one at a time for interviews. Our plan was to talk to each of them separately, hoping to get someone to shed light on how Hatfield's murder and Fiorino's death were connected.

Our first witness was a stripper named Mary. Mary worked at a club on "The Block," Baltimore's infamous red light district of that period. She was young, pretty, and more than a bit strung out. She lit cigarettes like a child playing with matchsticks. Her speech was slurred and spastic, a sort of East Baltimorese, greased and slippery.

"I don't know anything but what I was told," she offered as she nervously gulped down a cup of coffee.

She told me she shared the three-bedroom walk-up with two longshoremen named Irish Taggart and Eddie Mallon. Both were boozing, drugging, and partying enthusiasts. Fun lovers, as she described them, albeit overly passionate about it.

I wanted her to think about the period of time between Hatfield's murder and Fiorino's ending up in the ditch. So I asked if anything unusual had occurred in the apartment between those two events. Indeed she did recall something strange, a story as frightening as it was comical.

She told us she had been drinking with Eddie Mallon at an East Baltimore bar named the Flying Saucer. Later they ended up back at the apartment with a guy she didn't recognize.

She remembered going into her bedroom and then waking up later to find Mallon and a dancer named Frankie engaged in a heated conversation about the same guy, who was now sleeping on the floor, covered with a blanket. Or at least she thought he was sleeping.

"People were always stopping by, getting high," she explained, "so I thought he had just taken too many pills."

Now comes the comical part. Her roommates, Eddie and Irish, told her the guy was indeed high. In fact, Irish told her the man could not walk without help.

So the duo proceeded to grapple with the supposedly intoxicated stranger and gently guide him out of the apartment as Mary and Frankie watched. Never mind the somnolent guest had a massive bruise on his forehead. And forget about the bloodstained shirt Irish asked Mary to dispose of. And who cares that the inebriated visitor's head bounced off his chest like a rag doll as he was dragged across the carpet and into the hallway.

"They said he was tired," Mary insisted.

But it didn't take long for me to figure out who the guest was. Even before Mary ticked off the description I had a pretty good hunch who had been taking a dirt nap at the soon to be infamous apartment on Preston Street.

Phillip Fiorino.

It seems that the errant gunman had met his demise right there. Sometime, somehow, someone had shot him there in the apartment as Mary languished in a booze-induced haze. And then, two apparently quick-thinking longshoremen conjured up a story to get the body out of their abode without arousing her suspicion.

And in part it worked.

Mary seemed entirely convinced the zombie-like guest was simply stoned. She might have been lying, or was just dumb, but either way, she couldn't tell us for sure if the man we believed was Fiorino was actually killed in the apartment.

Still, even with Mary's vague recollections, we had the makings of a case. As a matter of fact, two other witnesses corroborated the story about the man wrapped in a blanket being escorted out of the apartment.

The same witnesses also told us they saw Mallon searching for Fiorino at the Flying Saucer the night he was shot. It was enough to haul both Mallon and Irish down to Homicide for questioning.

And that was the first time I laid eyes on him, the man who would threaten to kill me.

Like most sociopaths I've encountered, Mallon's potential for violence was not manifest in his physical appearance. In fact, he wasn't physically imposing at all. The *Baltimore Sun* described him as "baby faced," and indeed he was. But also, like many of those same killers, his eyes sort of beamed with recklessness. Two orbs blazing with hubris — not confidence, but savagery. There's a difference: truly, the man had no fear.

We questioned Mallon for four hours. He told us Irish and another man had come to his apartment the night Fiorino disappeared. He told us the last time he saw Fiorino was at the Flying Saucer. The only admission he made about anything suspicious occurring at 19 West Preston was how he had watched Irish wipe blood off a railing on the steps leading to the street.

That was it.

"Do you have any idea where the blood came from?" I asked.

"No I don't," he replied, diffident yet defiant.

But other information started to trickle in. We took the blanket wrapped around Fiorino's body and showed it to the building manager of 19 West Preston. He told us in no uncertain terms he had recently been inside Mallon's apartment and had seen the same blanket lying on a bed. We then got another statement from a friend of Fiorino's who said he told him a week before he died that he was doing a job for the union and would soon have "plenty of money."

And so a week later a Baltimore City grand jury indicted Eddie Mallon and Irish Taggert for the murder of Phillip Angelo Fiorino. The duo was charged with shooting Fiorino multiple times in their Preston Street apartment, then dumping his body in a ditch.

But the case was far from over. Hardly. The fireworks were just beginning.

To strengthen our case, we began to interview other witnesses. And soon a small-time operator named Tojo revealed an intriguing clue that would connect Fiorino's death back to Hatfield's murder.

Tojo was a working member of Baltimore's small-time criminal ensemble. He'd dabbled in everything: dope, fencing, gambling, you name it. But he was also an invaluable source for cops. Always up to date on the goings-on in the criminal undercurrents, Tojo was informed, an outlier with inside information.

He told us a story of his recent efforts to sell two pistols at a pool hall on Eastern Avenue. That's where he encountered a man I'll simply call "David" because he was never convicted of any crimes related to this case. "David" was interested in buying Tojo's guns. He was also hanging out with another man Tojo knew all too well: Guido Iozzi.

Tojo told us he offered the guns and that David was interested. So the pair met in an alley behind the bar, where David examined the merchandise. Pleased with what he saw, David later met Tojo at the Crown Steak House where he handed over 50 bucks and took the guns with him.

It was an important clue, because one of the guns Tojo sold David, a .22-caliber pistol, was the weapon used to murder Hatfield. A gun we had confiscated from 19 West Preston Street.

So we issued a warrant for David's arrest and brought him down to Homicide for questioning. Predictably, David denied everything. The gun purchases from Tojo, hanging around with Iozzi, the meeting at the Crown Steak House.

He wasn't defiant like Mallon however. In fact, you could see it in his face — doubt — a trembling bottom lip, an overly attentive gaze. He was hiding something in plain sight.

He asked us if he could make a phone call, so we took him out of the box and put him in a holding cell where he was given access to a phone. A few minutes later a sergeant watching the holding cells pulled me aside. He told me I wouldn't believe who David called.

Guido Iozzi.

Yup, the up until now innocent gun buyer got on the line and reached out to the city's most powerful union boss. I only overheard tidbits of the conversation, but David was panicked. He told Iozzi what we knew, about the gun purchase and the chance encounter with Tojo.

So I confronted him.

"Why'd you call Iozzi?" I asked.

"He's a friend."

I grilled him. I told him we had another witness who corroborated Tojo's story. I recounted Tojo's tale in exacting detail. Bottom line: we already knew what happened. And that was enough; he broke... sort of.

At first he told us a man named Jack gave him $800 to kill Hatfield. Cash he used to hire Fiorino to do the job.

We interviewed Jack and determined pretty quickly he had nothing to do with either murder. So we pressed David again. We told his lawyer he'd be facing life in prison, we already had enough to convict him. His only hope, cooperate.

So David broke again, and the story he told was a whopper.

"I was riding around with Iozzi," he said, "and he told me he was having problems on a Broadway job.

"What kind of problems?' I asked.

"Problems with Hatfield, he kept crossing the picket line."

Shortly after that conversation David told us a secretary working in Iozzi's office handed him a piece of paper with a list of names. First in line: Hatfield.

So David told us he spent a few weeks trolling the city's criminal hangouts looking for a man to scare the innocent shop steward. It was a mostly futile recruiting mission that led to deals with at least two petty thugs who eventually backed out. That is, until he found a man who left little doubt he could do the job.

Phillip Fiorino.

That's right, David told us he had almost given up when he read about Fiorino's acquittal for attempted murder. Once he located the potential hit man at the now infamous Flying Saucer bar, he hardly had to ask.

"I'm your man," Fiorino told David.

And so, shortly after David took Fiorino for a ride past Hatfield's house in his dark blue 1963 Pontiac Bonneville, he picked up the morning paper and read about a job not so well done.

The headlines were stark: Hatfield was dead. Shot and killed in his foyer.

"I was sick about it," David claimed.

Really?

I mean, he picked Fiorino because the guy had allegedly shot someone in the back of the head in an alley. He even supplied the apparent nutcase with a gun. Maybe he really did give Fiorino 500 bucks and a loaded weapon and told him only to rough up Hatfield. But apparently the gunman didn't get the message.

Still, with David's statement we had enough to charge Iozzi. It was a welcome break in the case that prompted my lieutenant to declare we'd landed "a big one."

But I didn't have the inclination, or time, to share my lieutenant's sense of accomplishment. In reality, charging an allegedly corrupt union boss was only the beginning of this unwieldy case, not a triumphant end. That's because as preparations for Iozzi's trial began, Eddie Mallon was beginning to reveal just how badly he wanted me dead.

I started this chapter with some thoughts on Baltimore's own homemade brand of brutality. Its venal, desperate, and scarily indiscriminate hold over all of us.

But even in a city so reflexively morbid, Mallon was a standout.

As I said before, he wasn't physically imposing. He was a wiry man coiled like a spring.

But there was a nervous, inconsolable spite in his eyes, a catlike gaze that tracked with feral precision.

And he was, as I stated before, fearless. Which I learned the day of his arraignment for the Fiorino murder.

I was sitting near the back of the courtroom waiting for the judge when Mallon was brought in. Plopping down at the defendant's table he surveyed the courtroom before spotting me. For a moment he just glared, sitting perfectly still while he fixed his gaze in my direction. Then, with his hands still cuffed, Mallon raised his fists in the air:

"Tabeling, I'm going to kill you!"

I was frankly stunned. I mean, I was used to getting nasty glares from suspects, and hard looks when I testified against them, but no one before had ever been so specific or open about their enmity. There I was, a cop sitting in court being threatened by a suspect. A defendant facing murder charges openly declaring I was next.

I was deeply troubled by his outburst, to say the least. This man had already killed, and now he had me in his sights. Most of all, I was worried about my family. I carried a gun, but my kids didn't. Who would protect my children if Mallon decided it was easier to go after them?

My superiors however told me I was overreacting. They said Mallon and his cohorts would soon be locked up. I was persuaded not to worry. Let justice run its course, they said. Simply wait for the rock-solid cases to play out, and Mallon would rot behind bars.

But it didn't happen that way. The law of entropy took over. As a matter of fact, everything went to hell so badly, it was like the world of justice had turned upside down just to shake me out if it.

First, Iozzi's case fell apart. And when I say fell apart, I mean it disintegrated right in front of me.

Now-famous attorney and Baltimore Orioles owner Peter Angelos had Iozzi's trial moved to the Eastern Shore. He argued his client couldn't get a fair trial in Baltimore due to adverse publicity. It was an ingenious move, though hardly necessary, because the case was over before it even started.

The state's key witness — in fact our only witness — recanted. That's right, "David" simply refused to testify. He denied all the statements he had made before. Right there on the witness stand, in front of the jury, he simply clammed up.

"I never heard about Kenneth Hatfield until I read in the papers that he got killed," he testified to a stunned courtroom.

I don't know why and was never given a reason for our star witness's decision to change his story. But the fact was, David simply didn't want to talk. He just went silent on the witness stand, and the case fell apart.

But a reluctant witness wasn't my only problem.

It's because Mallon's trial was also a bust. Despite testimony from the two women who watched Eddie Mallon and Irish Taggart walk a dead Phillip Fiorino out of the Preston Street apartment, along with the testimony of the building manager, Mallon was acquitted.

Acquitted! He was a free a man!

Mallon's defense attorneys picked our witnesses apart. The strippers were painted as wanton drug addicts and loose women. The building manager, a bumbling fool with a bad memory. Iozzi's acquittal also weighed heavily on the trial. We looked incompetent and unprepared.

It was a fiasco.

Still, it didn't matter who or what was to blame that Mallon was now back on the street. And so was Iozzi. Two murders and not a single person held accountable. The only person who suffered any sort of consequence for the mayhem which claimed two lives was our star witness David.

He was charged with perjury and for participating in a murder-for-hire scheme. But I believe that he too was acquitted.

However that's a small-time charge, and irrelevant. Unsolved murders breed more murders. Unrequited violence begets more violence. The most productive and important task of the criminal justice system is separating the most anti-social from the community.

And in this case, the system failed.

And so, Eddie Mallon was back in society — and I was forced into the unenviable position of constantly looking over my shoulder. I lived in a perpetual state of fear. True, he'd made intangible threats. It was a courthouse rant that could easily be written off as the ravings of a madman, or a frustrated perp.

But my gut was telling me his grumblings were far from meaningless. Something about the man himself, his intensity, his guilelessness, his dispassionate gaze, all sort of added up to a character who didn't just talk about violence, he acted.

But time passed. The case faded in my mind as new crimes presented fresh challenges. I continued to hone my skills as an investigator.

The Hatfield case taught me several valuable lessons. First, I needed to educate myself to build better cases. My takeaway from the failed prosecutions was the need to be smarter about the law, to understand potential witnesses better, and how to interrogate more effectively.

I also learned that a detective has to let go. Once the jury has rendered a verdict, you have to move on. You put on your best case, and leave the decision in the hands of the people.

And that's just what I did; I tried to put the case behind me. But it didn't work.

In May of 1969 I was attending a psychology lecture at Loyola University when a detective from Northern District walked into the classroom. He told me to head to District Headquarters and contact the commander, Major William Armstrong. The detective said an informant had told them a drug dealer was trying to hatch a plot to kill me.

"Do you know a woman who goes by the name of Butch Jerry?" the commander asked when I sat down in his office.

"I sure do," I replied. She'd been a reliable criminal informant for quite some time. In fact, she was partly responsible for some of my earliest, high profile drug busts.

"Well it seems she has information that Eddie Mallon is planning to kill you."

The commander told me Mallon asked her to set up a meeting with me. The plan: to take me out when I showed up.

According to Butch Jerry, Mallon believed I would go to any lengths to obtain information. "He said you'd do anything for a drug tip," she reported.

We met Butch at Homicide. She told us about the scheme, and that Mallon was holed up at the Holiday Inn downtown. So with a homicide detective named Harold Rose in tow, I got in the car and headed to a rendezvous with a man who had tormented me for three long years.

Driving to the hotel I was in a bad mood, to say the least. Time had passed since the Fiorino murder case. Good detectives move on, and I had. I thought it was over.

But it wasn't — far from it; and I was not happy to be back on Mallon's hit list.

But the tip also rekindled my frustration with the justice system. I'm not a proponent of filling up jails. But this guy belonged behind bars. He may not have been found guilty for murdering Fiorino, but he'd been in constant trouble since his acquittal. And now he was allegedly unrepentant enough to wait, plan, and carry out another murder.

Mine.

It was that moment when I decided I'd had enough. Mallon's beef with me was going to be settled one way or the other. His threats were going to stop.

His room was on the first floor of the hotel, so we had a pretty good view of what was going on inside. From our vantage point in the parking lot it was pretty clear Mallon and a friend were in the middle of an intense marijuana smoke-out. We could see the hemp-induced afterburn billowing out the first floor window. Seriously, I have to give the guy credit, he knew how to throw a party. I suppose that's how he kept his friends in tow, because there certainly wasn't much else about him to like.

With probable cause that illegal narcotics were being consumed, we entered the hotel room and found a stunned Mallon holding a wad of cash, a .38-caliber revolver and two ounces of marijuana.

"You're under arrest," I said as I spun him around and slapped on a pair of cuffs.

The grand jury indicted Mallon on the charge of conspiracy to commit murder, a charge that made headlines in the *Baltimore*

Sun but which also infuriated the prosecutor who had previously tried Mallon for the murder of Phillip Fiorino.

"Who the hell gave the okay to place that kind of charge on Mallon?" he fumed.

It was part of a pattern of skepticism of my concerns about Mallon's violent intentions that plagued the investigation. I had trouble getting anyone at Headquarters to take his threats seriously. I wanted a detail to protect my family, but a top level commander famously said I was overreacting.

"That Tabeling has a vivid imagination," he had told my superiors.

Fortunately, our investigation of Mallon's plan to kill me wasn't his only problem. Homicide detectives had been building an attempted-murder case against him for another bizarre plot — a botched scheme to kill a construction worker which made my encounters with Mallon appear downright friendly by comparison.

Turns out Mallon and three associates had dressed up like cops to pay a visit to a tradesman named John Owens. The hapless gang was apparently in search of narcotics, tipped off by Owens' disgruntled wife. During the home invasion, the gang ordered Owens to lie on the floor. Then one of them shot both of Owens' hands before pumping four bullets into his back.

Confident he was dead, the gang rifled through Owens' apartment and eventually left. But the boneheads had made a fateful mistake: Owens was still very much alive. In fact, the 34-year old contractor managed to crawl to a phone and call police.

Meanwhile I learned that Mallon had another alleged target on his criminal-justice hit list, prosecutor Charles E. Moylan Jr.. Not only was the guy after cops, but he seemed to have an ever expansive beef with the city's law enforcement establishment.

But three potential targets apparently weren't enough to keep Mallon busy. Just a few weeks later he was indicted again, this time for allegedly hiring a hit man to take out a downtown nightclub manager. Turns out detectives linked Mallon to a man named Gordon Williams, who police believe Mallon paid to kill the strip-bar manager, a man named Joseph Grieco.

Grieco had turned up dead on an abandoned weed-filled lot in East Baltimore a few months prior to Mallon's indictment for trying to kill me. The hired gun was paid $500 to shoot Grieco and dump his body in East Baltimore.

Needless to say it was an impressive trail of mayhem. Mallon had been so busy getting into trouble he had half the Homicide floor investigating him. And now the man who forced me to look over my shoulder for three years was set to answer for no less than three crimes of purported violence.

It was grim satisfaction to say the least.

And what happened? What was the outcome of these separate and distinct criminal cases? How was Mallon's alleged homicidal binge adjudicated?

Well, it wasn't.

He was found not guilty of each and every crime by reason of insanity.

I'm not kidding. During each trial a judge was presented with a psychiatric evaluation commissioned by Mallon's defense attorneys. Their determination: Mallon was insane. In other words, not criminally responsible for his behavior. Psychiatrists judged the sociopath-cum-union-man incapable of understanding the consequences of his behavior. Better put, he didn't know right from wrong.

Really? Go figure.

It was a stunning outcome. No, let me be more emphatic, it was a punch to the gut. It was like the sudden death of a friend or family member that leaves the bereaved survivors in shock, in a state of total denial. I just couldn't wrap my mind around the idea that Mallon was "not guilty."

I think I'm a relatively enlightened cop, but I still can't understand how a man who planned and coordinated several killings was too crazy to be held accountable. Maybe if he'd walked down the street brandishing a shotgun and picking off random strangers for no apparent reason, I'd understand. Maybe.

But not culpable for plotting, planning murder? Seriously?

It was devastating for both me and my family. I thought at the very least he would have been found guilty of something; at least one of the charges would have stuck. There certainly was enough evidence to convict. I sat through the trials, listened to the testimony. Hell, I even investigated one of the cases myself. But in the end, it didn't matter. Mallon was nuts, and so he was also "innocent."

But it gets worse.

Just three months after he was institutionalized Mallon's lawyers petitioned the court for his release. Their reasoning? Mallon was cured. I know this sounds crazy, no pun intended, but he was only "temporarily nuts." A doctor concluded after only four months in a state mental hospital that he was fit for freedom. I'm not kidding, not long after his breathtaking rampage of mayhem he was back on the streets.

But seriously, if the guy was crazy when he killed, how had he suddenly been cured? And how on earth could a jury and the medical profession work at such invidious ends? His attending psychiatrist even blasted the media for portraying Mallon as dangerous!

It was like the worst-case scenario for both me and the city. If the man was mentally ill and needed treatment, so be it. But he was provably a danger to himself and others. Putting him back into the community was foolhardy. He of all people needed to be locked away.

As I discussed in the previous chapter, mental health and its affect upon criminality is a topic that gets too little attention. Aberrant psychology drives a good portion of the chaos and violence on the streets of Baltimore. The truth is, sometimes people need help. And quite often in Baltimore, help is not often sought out.

But not necessarily because it doesn't exist. I mean, we have more world class hospitals than any other city in the country and probably the world. But I think there's a certain lack of self-diagnosis that comes with living in a community with extreme pockets of social dysfunction. Like all human behaviors, there's an aspect of relativism that drives our ability to recognize what's aberrant. So in a city with a couple hundred murders a year and even more shootings, what's "crazy"?

Still, in the end, the question of Mallon's state of mind is purely academic. But for me, it was a matter of life and death. I lived in fear, constantly concerned about the safety of my family. I'm not saying I looked over my shoulder every minute of every day, but his unexpected release cast a pallor over the city that for me never lifted. My job and my life were never the same again.

I was always conscious of the fact that being a cop didn't insulate me and my family from violence. Hardly. But I never anticipated that a man with such innate capacity for mayhem could so easily outmaneuver the city's justice system. Making it worse for me, when Mallon's lawyers petitioned the court for a review of his commitment to psychiatric care, the prosecutor who was assigned to argue on behalf of the state didn't even tell me about the hearing. In fact, he also didn't notify one of the key victims, the contractor who was repeatedly shot by Mallon and his crew.

It was an outrageous omission that still irks me to this day. In fact, it was such a blatant oversight it makes me wonder if it was purposeful.

I'll say this, Baltimore is like a small town; I've often wondered if Mallon had connections in law enforcement. If someone, somewhere was working to help him. It's not like Baltimore's criminal justice system can't mete out punishment. Despite public perception to the contrary, I've seen people put away for 10 years or more for simply being near a bag of crack.

But a man facing multiple murder charges simply walks out the door in a couple of months?

I don't have any direct proof, but why wasn't I notified about Mallon's hearing? Why was the victim also excluded from the proceedings? What was the rush to get Mallon back onto the street? Suspects are held without bail for far less serious crimes for years. Who and why was someone so anxious to set this guy free?

While things didn't work out for me in court, Mallon did however leave the state. He moved to Arizona in the early 1980s, a fact I learned when I received a phone call from a Mohave County sheriff in Arizona in 1992. Turns out Mallon had been arrested for money laundering and distributing methamphetamine. The sheriff was looking for some background information on his crimes in Baltimore as part of a pretrial investigation.

I tried to help him out. I visited Headquarters and rummaged through homicide files — but I couldn't find a shred of paper related to Mallon's past cases. Not a single file on Mallon remained! All records of him and his misdeeds had completely vanished.

In the long run though, it didn't matter. Mallon pled guilty and was sentenced to 15 years. I guess they don't mess around out West. Technically he would be out by now, but I haven't heard a thing about him since.

Still, the case and the man continue to haunt me; I suppose it's hard to forget a lunatic who threatens to kill you. It's one of those indelible memories, like a near-death experience or a car accident. Unfortunately, as much as I'd like to forget him, I can't, and I suppose I never will.

But more interesting than my own fears is what my run-in with Mallon taught me about Baltimore's ongoing lust for violence. What it really means to live under the constant threat of death. How a permanent pattern of chaos affects the psyche of an individual, and the community.

It's because violence, and the threat of it, begets terror.

It's a peculiar type of inner city terror propagated by people like Mallon which weakens the resistance of the community by engendering fear. The goal: to make us all feel vulnerable, and in the end acquiescent to criminality.

Consider a life where a simple walk to the corner store can turn into a death march. Can you imagine the psychological trauma, the neurological dissonance that would take hold in a person who lived under the persistent strain of instantaneous threatened death? Can any of us truly understand what it's like to exist in a community where there is no safe haven, no refuge from the wrath of others?

I think it is this state of terror which underlies much of the persistence of inner city violence. That's what I learned from my encounter with Mallon.

When my family was threatened, when my children's happiness and well-being were under siege from a madman, I wanted to strike back, I wanted to fight. I was jumpy and constantly vigilant. I was distracted and preoccupied. My job became secondary to my family's safety.

Truthfully, there were moments when I hated the job simply because I blamed it for putting my family in danger. Certainly there were times if I could have settled things with Mallon in a back alley somewhere, I would have taken my chances.

So I can only imagine how it feels to live in a poor, drug infested neighborhood. How the constant threat of violence must undermine a person's ability to be rational. Or even think ahead. How primal fear can motivate all types of self-destructive behavior. It's obvious to people who have lived with it. It's obvious to me.

I guess in a perverted sense I owe Mallon. In a way, he made me a better detective. I had insight into motives that other cops didn't. I really did understand the mind of a killer. A little bit of knowledge acquired through the often miserable slog of being a homicide detective that helped me along the way. An authentic perspective that served me well at times, but still lingers like an unpleasant aftertaste.

I guess if I were being honest, part of me wants to forget the truisms I learned about human nature from people like Mallon. The truths they teach us about our capacity for murder and cruelty. The knowledge of how easy it is for people to kill. And the unforgettable absoluteness of death.

I wish I could forget.

But I can't. I won't.

CHAPTER FIVE:
VENGEANCE IS NOT MINE

Black October and the
Murder of Turk Scott

Baltimore City, like most communities, has a split personality.

Within its borders, alleys and back-ways two parallel worlds exist side by side. Distinct civic selves, which become self-evident if you spend enough time immersed in both.

I know this because I was... and still am, a cop.

During my career as a lieutenant in Baltimore City Homicide, I often worked at a crossroads where the two worlds met. At the point where healthy productive communities and the criminal element clashed.

And while I worked dozens of murder cases and headed a variety of investigations, there is one case that to this day stands out as emblematic of the split personality that characterizes this town.

This case defined just how destructive the burgeoning drug war in Baltimore was to become, and just how complicated and costly fighting it would be.

It was a case that pitted the city against itself, and revealed how scars of divisive racial mistrust would be slow to heal — if ever they would heal at all.

It was a case that has all but been forgotten, although it sowed the seeds of many of the problems that hamper the effectiveness of our justice system even today.

It was also a story of a social movement that threatened to engulf the city in civil war, a vigilante movement which still remains, in part, a mystery.

I'm talking about the murder of Maryland State Delegate Turk Scott.

For most of my career I was an investigator, a detective, a person whose beat was the juncture of the aforementioned divide between the healthy and the unhealthy.

And when it came time for me to do my job, I tried, for lack of a better analogy, to be precise, and dogged. I mean methodical, hard-nosed, but within the law. I didn't fight violence by abandoning the law; indeed, I embraced it. I was "the law," so I acted like it. But I also acted within it.

That's been the mantra of my career — to follow, teach, and learn the law; it's the only way to police effectively.

To insure that cops remain peacekeepers and community builders simply demands they follow the law. Because when your job is to literally stand on the precipice of communal dysfunction, the law keeps the chaos at bay.

That's why the law has evolved. That's why it has to be followed.

And in the murder of James "Turk" Scott it was all I had.

AN UNWIELDY CASE AT SUTTON PLACE

It's a strange life, being at the nexus of all things violent. In the City of Baltimore, which numbered almost a million people when I was a homicide investigator, if someone found a body with a bullet hole in it they called us.

This is why a ringing telephone on the floor of the Homicide Division always had a sinister undertone. Like a perversion of Zuzu's wing-earning angels, when the bell chimed in our office, it meant someone had just met a violent end.

And if that call was from a homicide detective who was already on the scene of a murder to tell me I needed to "see this," I always knew there was something extraordinary attached to the body that lay prone and lifeless in some back alley or on a sidewalk of the city's urban hinterlands.

But nothing really prepared me for the murder, and its aftermath, that began with an early a.m. Friday the 13th phone call from one of my detectives who was standing in the parking garage at the Sutton Place Apartments on that morning in July 1973.

It was a grisly scene, yes.

A middle-aged African-American male lay on the parking garage floor surrounded by at least a dozen shotgun casings and spent slugs. The victim was dressed in a beige suit and paisley tie; blood-spotted entry wounds were visible on both his chest and lower leg.

But what caught my eye that morning, and what would ultimately draw this case into a firestorm of controversy was something else. Something you rarely see at a crime scene. I guess you could call it a message of sorts... and it wasn't subtle.

Strewn about the body like leftover litter from a raucous Irish wake were leaflets — dozens of them. All emblazoned with the name of a group that we had recently become aware of, but at that time had few clues to just how violent it would become.

Black October.

We didn't know much about the group at the time. Only vague rumors of a Westside-based vigilante movement that was targeting drug dealers. A phone call to the editorial desk of the *News American* and *The Sun* that a drug dealer had been murdered. Gunned down because he was poisoning the city.

But Black October was not my only concern. Because the murder victim sprawled on the floor of the parking garage was also a well-known public official — as I said before, State Delegate Turk Scott.

He was a politically connected bail bondsman, a consummate Baltimore insider who had been appointed to a seat in the Maryland General Assembly just months before.

And the plethora of shell casings scattered across the pavement made one thing clear, the killers were not simply trying to ambush the 48-year-old politician as he exited his car.

No, they had something entirely different in mind. The killers were trying to send a message.

Scott had recently been indicted by federal authorities for drug dealing: one count for conspiracy and three counts for distribution of heroin by attempting to bring 40 pounds of dope into the city. An indictment that made headlines across the country regaling the tale of a public official who was alleged to have been involved in the business of moving drugs through the City of Baltimore.

It was a drug case that confirmed everything I had suspected about the burgeoning and insidious illicit-narcotics business that was infiltrating the upper echelons of the city's political class. It was a growing underworld of incestuous relationships I had discovered while detailed to a special Narcotics Strike Force in the early 1970s (which I will say more about later).

There, lying on the pavement, his tie flipped over the back of his head lapping at the spent shotgun shell-casings that crept around his body like dead bugs, was the best example of what the growing influence of the drug trade had wrought: An elected official gunned down in the parking garage of his own home, adjacent to what was then Baltimore's most elite gentrified neighborhood, Bolton Hill.

And then there was the note from Black October.

Scrawled on the 8-by-11-inch sheets in brutish handwriting was the name of a group that had been lurking in the shadows of the city's undercurrent of violence. A loose organization that was rumored to be waging a vigilante war against the drug dealers in the city but whose real intentions remained as murky as the drug business they were alleged to be fighting.

It was a group that we had heard of but knew little about.

Allegedly named after an organized effort during the Vietnam War to aid heroin-addicted African-American soldiers, the group had come to our attention when another suspected city drug dealer was gunned down in broad daylight in Pimlico. Several days after that murder someone claiming to represent Black October called the *News American* newspaper and said the dealer was the first victim of their nascent war against drug dealers.

"He was killed because he was a drug dealer," the caller was quoted as saying.

And now, inscribed on the sheets of paper strewn across the Sutton Place parking garage was a short but succinct threat, a posthumous death sentence for Turk Scott and a warning of more trouble to come:

"These persons are known drug dealers," the flyers proclaimed. "Selling drugs is an act of treason. The penalty for treason is 'death'!! [signed] Black October"

And the unknown shooter or shooters also left a final statement, a broken piece of plastic bearing the name of a Sears automobile battery:

DieHard.

THE DRUG BUSINESS COMES OF AGE

As I said before, my job was to investigate murder, crimes of passion, dispassion and plain old vengeance. Baltimore City, as most people well know, has a penchant for violence.

People get killed violently for a whole variety of reasons. But in the 1970s, as I'm sure is true today, much of the killing was related to the business of selling illicit narcotics. Drug dealers killing drug dealers.

And I had a unique perspective on not just why, but how drug dealing was becoming the most destructive crime pattern in Baltimore. Because before I was assigned to the city's Homicide Unit, I was the only Baltimore City police officer tasked to the city's first special Narcotics Strike Force.

Formed in 1971 by then-State's Attorney Milton B. Allen, the Task Force was designed to combat the growth of the organized drug business in Baltimore.

Our job was not just to arrest drug dealers but to accumulate intelligence about the organizational structure of the business as a whole. We were tasked with fleshing out the big picture and identifying the major players.

And during a span of a few short years we did exactly that.

One of the biggest challenges we faced fighting drug dealers in the late 1960s and early 70s was keeping up with the growth of the organizations that had evolved hand in hand along with increases in the trade of drugs like heroin, cocaine and marijuana. As the drug trade expanded, so did the organizations.

But we needed intelligence, a clear and useful picture of who ran the drug business in Baltimore.

To achieve this we collected arrest data from the city's nine police districts and various narcotics units, and created a telephone tip line to receive information on drug dealers from the general public.

We also set up wiretaps and surveillance; we followed the players who soon emerged as the top organizers of the city's growing drug trade.

And through this work we were able to assemble a pretty coherent picture of how heroin and cocaine made its way from international locales to the streets and neighborhoods of Baltimore. And what we learned, which has been kept secret for decades, was pretty ugly.

It was ugly because in the 1970s, put simply, the heroin trade was not fronted by underground organizations or petty thugs. No. Thanks to our intelligence-gathering efforts we knew the exact opposite to be true.

The first thing to understand is that Baltimore was a major market for heroin even back then.

We didn't have estimates, but based on the size of some of the biggest local drug organizations, kilos of dope were being moved into the city on a daily basis. It was quite a bit of product, product that needed to be cut, packaged, and distributed every day.

The person who pushed product into the Baltimore supply chain for many of the organizations we tracked was a New York-based dealer named Frank Matthews, a/k/a "The Black Caesar."

Matthews was one of the biggest heroin traffickers on the East Coast. A legend, in fact, who gained notoriety by circumventing the Italian Mafia to buy heroin directly from the Cubans and Colombians and sell it in at least 20 cities up and down the East Coast.

Matthews would be what we call today a kingpin; he had the ability to deliver weight. And as his ability to import drugs directly to the East Coast grew, he found a ready market in Charm City.

We observed him in the company of some of the city's most infamous drug dealers, including "Little Melvin" — Melvin D. Williams, who played The Deacon on the TV show "The Wire" — and a man named Big Head Brother, who I will say more about later.

But what we learned from watching Matthews work, and how his supply was moved through the city, said quite a bit about how the drug business was changing — and the City of Baltimore along with it.

Because in the late 1960s and early 70s the drug business in Baltimore began to shape the urban landscape we see today.

The change was not simply in the obvious unsubtle exodus of residents that would begin a long, unending decline in population, nor the wholesale desertion of downtown — a fate the recently deceased Mayor (and later Governor) William Donald Schaefer spent his entire career trying to reverse by building lustrous Inner Harbor pavilions, stadiums at Camden Yards, and other tourist attractions.

The change perceptible on the street level, in the neighborhoods, was from an unseen tide of despair that began to slowly wash over once-stable communities in the form of a deviant and destructive business that had taken root in areas where the factories and jobs had left.

It was, in short, the ascent of organized drug dealing, and in particular heroin, that had begun to spread its deadly tendrils throughout the city. With it came the steady erosion that would soon begin to take apart Baltimore's bedrock of middle class communities piece by piece.

The growing business of distributing opiates gained momentum in the early 1970s and began the inevitable decline that has left us with the urban wasteland we see today.

To be sure, there were plenty of other factors that contributed to the urban decay that has become as legendary as Maryland's signature crab cakes. Unscrupulous landlords and blockbusting real estate speculators combined with the wholesale withering of the city's industrial base. And of course the simmering racial tensions between white and black residents that has always defined, in part, the city's psyche.

But the often destructive business that began its unabated takeover of Charm City was perhaps the strongest symptom of the sickness within. And it was my job as a detective in the Baltimore Police Department to fight it.

Unlike the seemingly more chaotic drug business of the new millennium, the process of dealing heroin in Baltimore City was not only well-organized in the early 1970s, it was also ingrained in the fabric of the community via legitimate business owners, and to be sure, a well-known soon-to-be-gunned-down politician at Sutton Place.

This I learned not only as the lead investigator of the special Narcotics Strike Force, but also as a homicide investigator for the city police department.

Through our work at the Narcotics Strike Force, we had identified the command structure of multiple drug organizations in

Baltimore City, traffickers that ran their operations from legitimate businesses.

Like the heroin ring at the Penn-Dol Pharmacy on Pennsylvania Avenue, for example. Or the drug gang headed by the owner of the Bear's Den on the 2800 block of Greenmount.

What was true then, and may well be true now, is that the business of drug dealing existed like a shadow cast over the everyday life of inner city Baltimore. It was like a subcutaneous infection, something that is in plain sight but stealthily hidden at the same time.

Still, it was the Turk Scott case that brought the ever-lurking business of illicit narcotics, with its insinuation into the fabric of city life, to the fore like never before. It was in a way emblematic of what we had learned in the Narcotics Strike Force:

The drug business was now the city's business.

THE LAW AND THE CASE

There is one thing you learn rather quickly investigating homicides: Everything changes when the case goes to trial.

It doesn't matter how solid a case you build, how many witnesses you find or how airtight the forensic evidence is. Once you enter a courtroom, your case is fair game. Defense attorneys and even the press can transform a straightforward case into a set of seemingly implausible facts.

This is why it is so vitally important for police officers to understand the law. If you don't know the law, you can't make the case.

Be careful of putting too much credence in the idea that law is an obstacle, a set of rules that gets in the way of rightfully prosecuting criminals. It's just not true.

Life is often messy, crime is virtually always messy. Think about it: when someone picks up a gun, points it at another human being and fires, what's left is a mess, blood and guts.

Something police call a "crime scene."

But the law is a way of taking something that is complicated and messy and giving it some sort of organizing principle, a structure for piecing together all different elements of a crime into a coherent case that gives the prosecutor the best possible chance of winning a conviction.

That's why the law is important, because it more often than not makes sense. And that's also why I've spent a lifetime since I retired as a Baltimore City police officer to teach it to as many officers as I can.

Because in the end, no matter how careful you are, when you end up in court, anything can happen.

I know it for a fact, because I've been there.

As I implied at the beginning, the killing of Turk Scott was nothing short of an execution, which we figured out quickly how the killers got done. But even as the case was coming together — I didn't know at the time — how we solved it would come under assault in ways that would overwhelm what we had uncovered.

The first thing we noticed was two distinct types of bullets: shotgun shell casings and spent slugs that, as I said before, surrounded the body.

The slugs appeared to be .38-caliber, the shotgun casings, 12-gauge.

In all, we found about half a dozen shotgun shell-casings and half a dozen spent slugs from the .38. It seemed that there might have been two shooters.

Next we examined the body, an examination that confirmed my initial impression that the shooter, or shooters, had more in mind than simply killing Scott.

You see, when you shoot someone in cold blood, depending on the motive, you stop when the victim appears to be dead; it's only common sense.

But in the Scott case, the gunman, or gunmen, didn't.

Scott had wounds all over his body, including several in his back, one near his kidney, which more than likely killed him, one in his chest, and one in the lower leg.

But when we removed his shirt, we found yet another gunshot wound at the base of his neck — more than likely a wound inflicted after he was already dead. The number of bullets and the postmortem wounds made it clear, the killers were sending a message.

So now we had an execution-style slaying of a public official who was under indictment for drug dealing. Further complicating the case, the specter of Black October loomed. What if, I thought at the time, this group really was preparing to wage war against drug dealers in the city? What if this was just the first in a series of planned killings?

To be sure, whoever was behind Black October wanted us to believe that Scott's murder was just the beginning.

So when a man claiming to represent the organization called the *News American* and took responsibility for the killing, we knew we had to solve this case quickly, otherwise whoever or whatever Black October was, could mushroom into something far worse.

OUR FIRST CLUE

Fortunately it didn't take long to get our first break in the case.

As I said previously, the crime scene was littered with Black October flyers that linked the murder of Scott to their war against drug dealers. But it was not just the flyers that gave us the lead we needed.

Not far from Scott's body, lying near a stairwell in the garage was a rolled up *News American* newspaper. From the start of the investigation it caught my attention not because it was odd for someone to toss a newspaper on the ground in a parking garage, but because it was slightly rolled in a way that could be used to conceal a weapon. As we canvassed the scene, our crime lab technicians took it, along with several flyers, for analysis.

And sure enough, just a day later they found prints. Seventeen points on the newspaper and 30 points on one of the Black October flyers.

Not just anyone's prints however, but 17-point handprints of someone well-known to me and other detectives, a young man who was connected to one of the city's most powerful African-American families and who I had encountered several years before.

Sherman Dobson. A manwas not your average suspect — hardly.

Sherman was the son of a minister and nephew of one of the most prominent African-American pastors in the City of Baltimore, Rev. Vernon N. Dobson, a Baptist minister and civil rights activist whose reputation extended well beyond Charm City.

His family lived in Ashburton, the most upscale African-American neighborhood, the same community in which current Baltimore Mayor Stephanie Rawlings-Blake grew up and still lives.

They had influence and power. The type of influence and power that black churches wield in Baltimore, then and now.

I had encountered Sherman Dobson six years earlier in the most unlikely place, in the cafeteria of a city high school.

It was a steamy afternoon in 1967 when I was working plain-clothes in the Northern District. I was called to a disturbance at Baltimore Polytechnic Institute, which in 1952 had become the first public high school in the city to racially integrate its student body. More than 200 students were staging a "sit-down" to protest against the Vietnam War. We were called in to calm things down.

But as I and another city police officer entered the cafeteria, the students locked the doors. Suddenly we found ourselves trying to mitigate tensions inside a claustrophobic school lunchroom filled with unruly teens.

One of the leaders of the student protest was Sherman Dobson. He was obviously bright, and certainly had the other students under his sway. He approached, catching me off-guard by instantly giving me a nickname.

"Hey! Clark Kent," he called to me as I stood in the cafeteria. (I never did find out precisely what he meant by calling me by Superman's alter ego, although some people say I looked a bit like the comic book character back then.)

We managed to persuade the students to ratchet down the protest, but my encounter with Sherman stayed with me.

And now we had his fingerprints on at least two pieces of evidence from the Turk Scott crime scene.

Plus we uncovered even more evidence pointing to Sherman.

Witnesses said they saw two men lingering near the parking garage just before Scott was gunned down. But they also reported seeing a red Royal Cab driving from the scene after Scott was shot.

And that got our attention.

That's because not one, but two cab drivers had reported being hijacked by three masked men in and around the Ashburton area in the days leading up to the shooting. One kidnapped days

YOU CAN'T STOP MURDER

before the shooting, and the driver of another Royal Cab the same morning Scott was shot.

Even more intriguing, one of the drivers, who we believe was carjacked as part of a practice run several days before Scott was killed, got a good look at one of his captors.

The driver told us he picked up three young men in the 900 block of Druid Hill Avenue near Druid Hill Park and that once inside the cab the three men brandished weapons and forced him to drive to a deserted area of the park.

There, the trio forced him out of the cab and handcuffed him to a tree. Fortunately for us, one of the assailants stayed behind while the others took off with the cab. Later, the driver said he could identify the kidnapper who stayed behind.

One of my detectives created a photo array for the cabbie, an array which later would become a basis for an appeal of a conviction stemming from the driver's kidnapping, an array which included Sherman Dobson.

And sure enough, the cab driver identified the man who watched while he was handcuffed to a tree as none other than Dobson himself.

THE STRANGEST SEARCH

Remember at the beginning of this story I said that everything changes when a case goes to trial?

It's a statement born out of experience.

We had evidence, hard evidence that implicated Sherman Dobson. Fingerprints from two pieces of evidence found at the murder scene and a solid identification by the cab driver who had been carjacked at gunpoint just days before Scott was killed.

With this evidence, and a tip from an informant that Sherman kept an array of weapons at his family home, all we needed was to conduct a search.

One of the most important and least understood aspects of any investigation is the obtaining of a warrant and the conducting of a proper search. The Fourth Amendment to the Constitution protects us from unreasonable search and seizure. It is a logical and productive safeguard.

A safeguard that has to be respected.

Yet quite a few cop shows these days try to depict the Fourth Amendment as an obstacle, something that prevents police from catching criminals, or provides lawbreakers with a myriad of technicalities to evade punishment.

However in my opinion, as a lifelong police officer and experienced investigator, nothing could be further from the truth.

The Fourth Amendment not only protects citizens, it protects police as well. Imagine if we could simply barge into any home or open any door in a non-emergency situation without so much as a calling card. That we could simply stop people on the street whenever we felt like it, or break down the doors of people's homes simply because we didn't like them.

That's what life would be like without the Fourth Amendment. The police would be hated and feared by everyone, with no cooperation — and with good reason.

But there's more.

Writing a search warrant is not only a requirement of the law, it is a task that ultimately makes for a stronger case. It helps cops organize their thoughts and evaluate evidence before they go knocking on a door, a vital step in case-building that makes us better prepared when we finally go to trial.

Remember, in order to preserve citizens' individual freedom to move about, or right to come and go as they please, there has to be some protection in place to ensure it.

A cop with a gun and a badge is an ordinary person with extraordinary powers. If he or she could stop you without probable cause or enter your home without a warrant signed by a judge, it would make the core right of democracy — the freedom to come and go as you choose — impossible.

Also, and almost as important, it is really not that difficult to persuade a judge to sign a warrant. In my career I was never turned down, in part because several well-respected judges took the time to teach me how to write a proper warrant.

And never were those lessons more important for me than in the case of Sherman Dobson, because the search that we executed during our investigation ended up consuming the case at trial and having a pivotal impact upon the outcome.

With the evidence we had and the tip from the criminal informant, we didn't have any trouble obtaining a warrant from the judge. The only thing I was worried about was that Sherman would get wind of our plans and hide the evidence.

Fortunately that did not happen.

TWO STORIES, SAME SEARCH

When we knocked on the door of the Dobson home in the heart of Ashburton in Northwest Baltimore, it was the estimable Rev. Harold Dobson, Sherman's father, who answered the door, along with Sherman's uncle Vernon.

"I have a search warrant," I told the reverend. "And we're going to search the house."

Both men were polite and respectful. In fact, Rev. Vernon Dobson escorted me through the house personally.

Just for the record, I had roughly seven officers with me, two other detectives and four uniformed cops.

Inside a closet in Sherman's room we found a .38-caliber handgun and ski mask.

Downstairs in the basement we found a shotgun hidden behind a shelf. And we also found shotgun casings and bullets for both guns. It was certainly enough evidence to raise serious suspicions about Sherman's involvement in Turk Scott's killing.

We handed over the guns to the Crime Lab. But after a series of ballistic tests, our technicians concluded that neither of the weapons could be linked to the shell casings found near Scott's body.

Nevertheless, while we were not able to connect either of the guns to the shooting, our search would certainly have implications for the case, which I will delve into later.

Still, armed with the fingerprints and the cab driver's identification, we were able to get a warrant for Sherman Dobson's arrest.

When he arrived on the Homicide floor, he was his usual confident self. He took one look at me and said, "I remember you, Clark Kent." But that was all he said. Before I could even ask what he meant by the nickname or have a polite conversation with him, he had a lawyer.

But even with a suspect in custody and what seemed like a pretty solid case, I knew we were in for a rough trial. When you arrest a member of one of the city's most prominent African-American families, a son and nephew of two preachers, you're going to have a fight on your hands.

Little did I know it would be a knock-down, drag-out brawl.

A TRIAL WITH TWISTS

Looking back on the trial of Sherman Dobson, former city prosecutor Milton Allen, Maryland's first African-American state's
attorney, had a simple lament about the price he paid for the
drama that unfolded inside Baltimore's Clarence M. Mitchell Jr.
Courthouse in 1973.

"Steve, the Dobson case cost me the election," he lamented years
later. (Allen was defeated for reelection in 1974 by William A.
Swisher, who eight years afterward was himself defeated by later
Baltimore Mayor Kurt L. Schmoke.)

It was a time of exacerbated racial tension in Baltimore in the
decade following the assassination of Rev. Martin Luther King
Jr., a period when blacks and whites alike retreated to their own
neighborhoods as they had in the years preceding integration.

I think Allen was right. In a sense, the trial of Sherman Dobson
was a watershed moment for the city's criminal justice system, a
notorious case so thick with politics it was hard to breathe in the
courtroom. Because from the onset of the trial the defense made
it crystal clear that the defendant, Sherman Dobson, wasn't the
one who was on trial at all. It was in fact us, the Baltimore City
Homicide Division. I'm not overlooking the fact that our work,
to a certain extent, is always on trial. But in this case the defense
took that strategy to an extreme that I have never experienced
before or since in all my years as a cop.

Let me say before I go any further that I respect the decision
of the jury in the Dobson trial, along with the right of a man
accused, to defend himself. Everything I write here is a matter of
fact reported by the media and recorded in court transcripts. My
only complaint is I believe politics overwhelmed the proceedings
to the point that what went on in court had very little to do with
the evidence against Sherman Dobson, and everything to do with
painting the Baltimore Police Department in the worst possible
light.

When I say politics, I mean the tensions between the Police
Department and the community. That's because it was the dra-

matic testimony of Sherman's uncle, Rev. Vernon Dobson, that turned the proceedings into an indictment of us, the cops. An entirely different version of events told in open court which still puzzles me to this day.

Reverend Dobson's testimony centered on our aforementioned search of his home just before we charged and arrested Sherman. But what he told the court had little resemblance to what I did that evening.

Instead of the four uniformed officers and two detectives accompanying me that evening, Reverend Dobson said there were over 150 cops stationed outside his Ashburton residence long before we entered.

And instead of what I recall as an orderly search of his residence in the presence of the reverend the entire time, he told the jury a "pug nose" officer had run up the stairs to Sherman's bedroom.

Even more astounding to me, was Reverend Dobson's claim that we had broken into the basement before knocking on his front door, and planted guns in the cellar. Kind of ridiculous, given that the guns we allegedly planted turned out to have nothing to do with the case.

But the strategy behind all this appeared to be conflicting testimony that was pretty easy to figure out.

To say that the atmosphere in the courtroom was tense would be like saying that standing on the corner of Biddle and Gay Streets in the middle of a hot August afternoon is a little "uncomfortable."

Not only did the supporters of the Dobson Family pack the courthouse daily, the press touted headlines each and every day of the trial. So as the Rev. Vernon Dobson sat on the stand accusing us of planting evidence and of showing up like a small army on his front lawn, the accusations made headlines, and the headlines weren't good.

Never mind that his testimony conflicts with what I believe happened, which was a perfectly legal and orderly search.

That wasn't the point.

What Reverend Dobson's testimony accomplished was to put the focus on us, not his nephew. And it was a strategy that paid off.

Because for nearly half a day I was on the stand. Sitting in the witness box, I had to read the run sheets for uniformed officers and patrol cars for every single district in the city to recount what every officer was doing. Every call for service, every dispatch, every movement of a patrol car, all to disprove his claim by showing that it just wasn't possible 150 officers could have been standing outside his house.

So there I sat for hours reading one activity sheet after another as the jury seemed to melt into a semblance of disinterested boredom. One by one, I read off the calls for service, car stops, and other mundane deployment details. Hour by hour I recounted the whereabouts of each and every police officer that donned a uniform that day. Minute after minute of tedious testimony, sitting in the witness stand, grilled by the prosecutor, poring over run sheets while the jury sat stupefied.

But in the end, it didn't matter.

Even though one of the cab drivers identified Sherman as his kidnapper, and even with the expert testimony from our Crime Lab technician that proved the prints on the newspaper and Black October flyers found at the scene were Sherman Dobson's, a Baltimore City jury found him not guilty of killing Turk Scott.

Looking back, there is no doubt in my mind why the jury acquitted him. Put simply, politics. For whatever reasons, the African-American citizens of Baltimore decided that the son of the city's most prominent religious family was not going to jail.

But not because he didn't shoot Turk Scott.

No, I think they decided it didn't matter. In the end, in the minds of the jury, justice was served. A drug dealer was dead. No reason to ruin the life of a promising young man from a powerful family. So in the end, politics trumped justice.

And while Sherman was found guilty of kidnapping and robbing the city cab driver who identified him, the verdict in the killing of Scott was a stunning blow to justice in this city. And I say that not just because I worked on the case.

Sherman Dobson was a troubled youth, dangerous to himself and others.

Several years after he was acquitted of Scott's murder he shot a police officer in Baltimore during a robbery. The officer survived, but the fact remains that Dobson was willing to point a gun at a cop, and at least in that instance, fire.

But what made me most uneasy about Scott's murder trial was the role politics played in its outcome.

As a cop I understand how politics influences what we do, how sometimes the will of an aggrieved constituency influences the process of policing.

Guilt or innocence is often a matter of perspective. Even the worst criminals don't think of themselves as bad, or even at fault. And even when evidence is solid, and proof hard to refute, personal prejudice can often trump the facts.

But there is a time for politics and a time to mete out justice. In the process of deciding guilt or innocence the meddling of politics that has nothing to do with guilt or innocence can render a justice system dysfunctional.

Ultimately the jury acquitted Sherman, and in the end I can't argue with a jury. But I think the acquittal was more a rejection of police tactics, not the evidence itself.

Which is why I focus so much of my attention on the law. Why I spend so many hours learning it and teaching it to other cops.

It's like an insurance policy for justice. If you want to insure that personal prejudice and partisan politics cannot corrupt the process of deciding right and wrong, follow the law.

Somebody killed Turk Scott, a man who was not a stellar citizen. In fact, he represented the deepest and most troubling form of corruption. The kind of rot from within I believe stunts the efforts of honest, hard working city residents to turn Baltimore back into a thriving, industrious metropolis.

Let's remember, the system was working when Scott was gunned down. The feds had Scott under indictment. He was facing serious charges. More than likely, he had stopped dealing drugs.

But his murder was vigilante justice, nothing less, nothing more. An act that sounds good in theory until someone with a gun shows up on your doorstep to act as judge, jury and executioner.

People that kill without compunction are dangerous. They do not discriminate. That's why this murder needed to be solved, for the good of the community, for the protection of everyone.

But in the courtroom, the good of the whole was not served, in my opinion. Guilty or not, politics won out, and a police officer later had to pay the price for that lapse in communal judgment, with a bullet in his chest.

Dobson appealed the kidnapping verdict. He argued that the photo array was prejudiced because he was the only suspect in the array wearing glasses.

The appeals panel sent the case back to Circuit Court for a new trial; however the state chose not to retry it.

But the more important effect of the outcome of the trial is best expressed in Milton Allen's lament — that he lost his next election because of this trial. In other words, for pursuing justice, he was turned out of office. Since then, the much more politicized State's Attorney Office has struggled to right itself.

And what of Black October? If their motive really was to rid the street of drug dealers, did they succeed?

No, they certainly did not succeed, and for a very simple reason.

Violence, no matter the intent behind it, doesn't heal. In fact, it only creates new wounds, new cases that have to be pursued, and a new batch of bodies in the morgue.

I can't say I blame the black community for feeling besieged by the growing tendrils of the drug trade. I can't even say I blame the people who lived with the ever growing disruption of an increasingly entrenched drug business for trying to take matters into their own hands, if that's what Black October was really all about.

I don't blame them, but I certainly can't condone it.

Because there was something else lost as a result of Turk Scott's death that never made headlines. Secrets untold that show why vigilante justice is not only morally wrong, but ineffective.

Scott never had his day in court.

In other words, the person who could have shined a light on the cancer of corruption the drug business was inflicting upon the city's productive community never got to testify. The opportunity to expose how the city's criminal element was infiltrating Baltimore's power structure via the illegal drug trade ended with a dead body in a parking garage.

Even after Scott's murder people I knew at the FBI wouldn't talk about the case. Whatever secrets he had he took to the grave.

To be sure, Scott was not the only suspected drug dealer Black October took credit for murdering. Shortly after his death the group claimed killing two other known dealers. The city was, to say the least, on edge.

So the police had to act: We identified at least six people who we believed were involved with the group and put a 24/7 tail on them. We didn't have enough evidence to bring charges, the intent was simply to let them know we were watching.

After several weeks of surveillance the young men we believed were involved in the Black October killings disappeared. I know it sounds odd, given that we were watching, but one by one they slipped away and vanished, and never returned to Baltimore, at least not on my watch.

Afterwards, the killings stopped, and Black October seemingly ceased to exist.

A STORY UNTOLD

Or did it?

When I started writing this book, I wanted to know more about Black October. How and why it came into being. I just wasn't satisfied that this so-called vigilante group which ran drug dealers out of town simply vanished.

Seems odd, I know. Why would the cop who investigated the group, need to know anything? Wouldn't I have already figured it out?

But the truth is, cops tend to hew to the case and the evidence in front of them. My focus then was on the murder of Turk Scott. I didn't have the time or inclination to investigate Black October.

So my co-author Stephen Janis was able to get in touch with someone who had firsthand knowledge of the group, and the following is what we learned.

(Just a caveat, there is no way to verify this information. While much of the account makes sense to me, I have no way to know how accurate it is. For whatever reason, Black October is a sore subject in the city's African-American community. A dangerous secret on the one hand, and a memory that has already faded from the collective mind of a community facing more pressing crises.)

Our source told us the Black October movement began in the Baltimore City School System: Several African-American female students from Eastern High School had tried to form a black consciousness group. But an administrator called police and the students were arrested.

The arrest turned into a protest at Northeastern District Headquarters. A protest which stimulated discussion and anger amongst students who had joined in protest and who believed the police were targeting their right to self expression.

There was also a growing concern amongst young black teens that the drug business was destroying the black community. Many of the young people attracted to the black consciousness movement believed the narcotics trade was intentionally situated in their communities to wreak havoc. To address these concerns, Black October was formed to fight back.

As to the moniker, the source told us the group was named after Black September, a Palestinian liberation movement which fought an insurgent war in the 1960s. We were advised to watch the beginning of the 1966 war film "The Battle of Algiers" if we wanted to better understand the impetus that drove Black October to kill drug dealers.

The movie recounts the war between the native Algerian population and French colonialists. As the insurgents plan to retake their country, they purge the city of drug addicts and prostitutes. It's a prelude to reinvigorating the populace and reasserting national identity.

The source offered no firsthand knowledge of Black October's more nefarious activities. Only that many in the various black communities shared their antipathy towards drug dealers, and that the murders were perceived as a kind of street justice.

That was all we could learn about Black October. In a way it helps me to understand their motivations, even if I don't agree with their methods. But it also raises so many other questions.

That's why I often think about the case, about Turk Scott and the secrets he left behind on the floor of that parking garage. I think about it because I witnessed a piece of Baltimore history that to this day remains unresolved in my mind.

Like so many of the cases I worked on and recount in this book, the criminal side of Baltimore's psyche won a partial victory simply by silencing Turk Scott.

True, people went to jail; and true, Black October's campaign of vengeance ceased. But in the end, we never heard from the man who knew the truth. Our community never had the chance to cauterize the wound that the drug business was inflicting upon the city by outing him.

By making him talk, by learning the truth, maybe we could have struck a serious blow against it. It was an opportunity lost.

I guess I'll just have to live with that. But what bothers me even more, is... so will the people of Baltimore.

CHAPTER SIX:
THE FOREVER WAR

The Dismantling of the
Narcotics Strike Force

YOU CAN'T STOP MURDER

There are days, which are few, when I return.

I take a left off Greenmount Avenue onto Biddle Street. A few blocks east, I make a sharp right onto a street that parallels Wilcox, where I grew up, and drive a short distance past the trash-filled alleys that divide the backyards of aging row homes. I park next to a broken sidewalk that sprouts weeds like leather daisies in the hot summer sun.

For lack of a better word, I'm "home."

Not home as I remember it, but the neighborhood I used to call home. My childhood home, the place where I played stickball, picked fights on the corner, and plied my own brand of smart-ass until it became an ingrained personality trait.

Sometimes I get out of my car just to contemplate the concrete shells that line the streets. The crumbling façades. And the empty, frameless windows that stare back at me. Vacant eyes, hollow and dusted.

There are vestiges of a vibrant community here too. St. James Church stands resolute as ever, a solid red brick backstop for the Institute of Notre Dame which remains a vital place of learning. Daily its courtyard filled with uniformed schoolchildren.

Around the corner, St. James School for Boys, where I played trumpet in the school band and drank beer at the age of 15 in the basement after a hot workout, still stands as it has for over a hundred years.

But when I stray beyond these few blocks, the oasis in this desert of rundown realty ends. Soon the ragged remnants of Baltimore's past become nearly accusatory. Once populated with the families that were the heart of the city's proud industries, only ghostly side streets now remain, denuded of life. Where we once used to play, only dreary alleys abide, moldering silently with rats, trash, and garbage.

Honestly, as I walk it's the emptiness that bothers me the most.

Like an endless row of unmarked graves, hollow homesteads bereft of any trace of the people who lived and died here.

Sometimes I just wander, walking the streets like a beat cop seeking to revive the life of a community in a rusty old mind. I spot a stray cat crouched in the shadow of a derelict bicycle, the skin of an ancient baseball shed alongside a cast-off shoe.

How could this happen? How could things fall apart so completely on my watch? I became a cop to preserve and protect the community. And now large swaths of the city I served for nearly 30 years are vacant and forgotten, like a weary battleground which stands in abeyance, to me. A reminder of an unsettling truth: We failed. Not just me — us.

Standing amid the squalor, I can't help but feel sorrow. How did we get it so wrong that these days the only signs of life in the neighborhood I used to call home are rats and restless shadows?

I don't pretend to have the answers. I played just a small role in the real drama of this city's decline. As both a street cop and an investigator, I'd like to think I did my best to turn back the onslaught of drugs and violence that has left behind so little.

But that doesn't mean my work didn't add to this story of decline. We all made mistakes, and the biggest one that comes to mind is a mistake that continues to influence the present. But perhaps it wasn't just a mistake; that's oversimplifying. Let's call it a missed opportunity.

The Baltimore Narcotics Strike Force.

I can imagine you're chuckling now. Laughing at the bureaucratic instinct of a cop who thought he could fix the city with a committee. Someone who believed that with the right mix of might and guts, laws and resources, we could repair a community already on an unwavering path of dissolution.

Laugh if you want, because I believe in part it's the truth. I believe had the Narcotics Strike Force been allowed to finish its work, then we would have made progress by rooting out some of the worst repercussions of the growth of the drug business in Baltimore before they took hold. A business that no doubt contributed to the mess we see today. And more importantly, we could have demonstrated a better way to police the narcotics business and have avoided an even bigger mistake.

The drug war.

The decades-long battle against the human predilection to alter the mind. The ongoing struggle to abate the use of a myriad natural and synthetic substances that fall under the purview of the country's law enforcement community.

Yes, I know I'm not the first cop to take a swipe at the war on drugs. LEAP, or Law Enforcement Against Prohibition, has thousands of members. Privately, I know many of my fellow retirees have doubts about it. Yet even our current top prosecutor in Baltimore, Gregg Bernstein, is trying to reduce the penalties for possession of small amounts of marijuana to free up the courts and allow his prosecutors to focus on more serious crimes.

So certainly I'm not the first cop to complain about it.

But as I look back at the opportunities missed and how this so-called war has evolved, I wish more than anything that we'd given a bit more thought to what we were doing. That perhaps we should have debated how exactly to fight the onslaught of illicit drugs into cities like Baltimore. Maybe instead of instigating a war against ourselves, we could have come up with an effective means to lessen the toll, and the burden that the use of narcotics levies on all of us.

Because the underlying philosophy of the war on drugs, and the implications of it, is why our country is in the unenviable position of having prisons filled beyond their stated limits, overtaxing of the court systems, and empty cities like Baltimore. It was a philosophy that all began with a word.

War.

From that fateful word all the inept characterizations and misguided policies grew. It was, in a sense, a potent symbol of a bad strategy. A word that eventually defined a transformation in policing that not only changed the job, but altered the philosophy that has defined modern policing for over a century.

Because, quite frankly, cops don't "fight wars," cops aren't warriors or soldiers. Put simply, police enforce the law, and there's a difference between the former and the latter. Cops make arrests, soldiers kill.

Enough said.

It's an idea that pushed the philosophy of policing off the path of investigation and enforcement and onto the road of fighting. And nothing exemplifies better what could have happened if we had avoided becoming street warriors than my work on the city's Narcotics Strike Force.

The Narcotics Strike Force was an entity entirely different from the drug-war bureaucracy that exists today. Our charge wasn't to fight. Instead, we were tasked to gather intelligence, to figure out just how deep and entrenched the drug business was in Baltimore. Our job was to investigate, prosecute, and liberate by using the law.

But before I tell the tale of the peculiar group that inhabited a few nondescript offices in the city's Clarence Mitchell Courthouse more than 40 years ago, let me relate the story of a drug arrest that reveals in a nutshell the real dilemma confronting a narcotics cop fighting this so-called war on drugs in the 1970s. It was an arrest that evinced all the politics and pitfalls of why this war was actually a running farce.

In late 1971 I was working my way back into the good graces of the department by busting my butt to make drug arrests. Because the burgeoning drug business had become a major nuisance, the commissioner of police signed a general order which gave permission for drug units to cross district boundaries.

(For those who don't know, the Baltimore Police Department is composed of nine districts organized by geographic areas, for example, Western District, Eastern District. They are distinct geographical territories — jurisdictions — guarded fiercely by commanders).

I wanted to take advantage of the opportunities afforded by the new freedom and prove I could do the job. Fortunately, I had an excellent informant and, thanks to the new focus on drug arrests, a new asset in my squad: I had recently traded one of my detectives for a cop from Washington, D.C.

The thinking was that a fresh cop was a clean cop. Working with my chief inspector, the transplant and my squad were notching so many arrests that territorial friction was starting to interfere with our progress. In other words, rival commanders didn't like my squad making arrests in their districts.

My informant told me she had found a new coke dealer moving pretty decent weight in an apartment complex on St. Paul Street. This alleged cocaine dealer was brazen and confident, running a veritable walk-in shop in the heart of the city's hip Mount Vernon neighborhood.

So I gave the undercover detective marked $50 bills to make what's known as a "controlled buy." And sure enough, with my CI in tow, the detective walked into the apartment, bought $100 worth of coke, and left.

Of course, buying drugs in Baltimore's Mount Vernon neighborhood, in the shadow of the city's Washington Monument, is hardly noteworthy. What made this case stand out is who was selling the drugs.

Because when we served the warrant and raided the apartment, the man who walked out in handcuffs was none other than the governor of Maryland's director of finance for law enforcement, the chief accountant for all of the state's police agencies.

Seriously, a high-level state official who managed the proverbial checkbook for cops was selling cocaine, heroin, methamphetamine and marijuana in his Mount Vernon apartment. Worse yet he had in his possession the marked $50 bills I had given to the undercover detective.

Still, with hard work and a well-executed investigation we'd made a pretty big bust. A powerful state official at the nexus of law enforcement engaged in criminal conduct, a government-paid crook perpetuating and participating in the drug business.

It was also an important lesson on just how insidious the drug trade was in Baltimore.

The more drug arrests I made, and the deeper I penetrated into the layers of distribution, the more I realized making a dent in the drug business would require confronting some uncomfortable truths about human nature that have little to do with policing.

It was clear you could only get so far by busting kids on the corner. The real game, the place where the drug business was most corrupting, was inside the apartments like the drug den on St. Paul Street. Not necessarily due to the drugs themselves and the toll they took on individual lives, but the fact that the money and the influence which fueled the sale of illicit drugs could ensnare a man with seemingly so much to lose. If he felt inclined to sell drugs, then why not cops? Why not teachers? Why not a state delegate?

Again, I don't want to sound naïve. It makes sense that an underground economy growing so quickly would spread its influence beyond the street-level dealer. It also makes perfect sense that an expanding drug market would need massive coordinated planning and logistics to infiltrate every corner of the city so effectively. But as a cop, I make judgments based upon evidence, concrete tangible facts. I need to see it firsthand before I totally believe it. And with this case I was just beginning to grasp how the culture of the drug game could be even more corrupting than the breadth of the commerce it supported.

What I mean is that, yes, the millions of dollars in profits would be so tempting, almost impossible to resist for a community whose traditional source of wealth — manufacturing — was in a long tortuous decline. In fact, it was almost like the fortunes of the city's legitimate economy and the illicit alternative were on a long collision course.

But the arrest of this man, a well-paid state official firmly ensconced in the community's political power base, also revealed that the drug business could lure people simply by the appeal of its cultural power. The fact that drugs and getting high complemented and heightened the Dionysian taste of a modern-day city made it an even more tempting preoccupation. It seems the forbidden nature of drug dealing itself was the ultimate draw, at least in this case.

That's why I felt good about the arrest. We had landed a big fish through solid police work. But more importantly for me, I felt I was learning about the dizzying scope of the drug business. Through this case and many others, I was gaining insight and connecting the dots.

But the very next day I got a rude awakening from my wife, literally.

"The commissioner's office just called. He wants to see you," she said.

I was pretty sure it wasn't to pat me on the back.

As I describe in other chapters of this book, Commissioner Donald Pomerleau was blunt to a fault. He never minced words, or let you down easy. Still, his tirade that morning was high-octane even for him. He was like a pit bull on meth, seemingly incapable of an even-tempered remark. And the focus of his wrath was my apparent incompetence and... the arrest.

That's right, the arrest.

"Goddamn you, you don't have any sensitivity to politics," he stammered. "Don't you know what it means to me when someone in the Governor's Office is arrested?"

"Commissioner, I notified the lieutenant."

"I don't want to hear nothing from you! Not a thing from you!" he screamed.

Of course, neither my lieutenant nor the colonel said a word in my defense: I was on my own. The pit bull commissioner baring his teeth, and me, the allegedly bungling sergeant, making a quick exit before he erupted again.

I was in the dead center of a colossal mess.

So I walked back to my office and wrote out all the reports due as a result of the bust. But truthfully it was hard to concentrate.

I understand politics. I know if you're pursuing a high-level target you need approvals. I realize investigating cases involving government officials or cops requires a modicum of caution and a heaping helping of communication. But Pomerleau's outrage was blatantly corrupt. A legitimate drug arrest under fire because the laws don't apply to people who work for the governor? And even more troubling, a man working with law enforcement dealing heroin and cocaine as a side business? What was the commissioner really telling me? That drug laws only apply to poor, politically irrelevant people?

Of course he was: Welcome to the real drug war.

The commissioner never said another word to me about it. And by the time the "esteemed" member of the governor's staff ended up in court, the fix was in.

Even though we had made a legitimate, controlled, hand-to-hand buy from the suspect and confiscated significant quantities of drugs from his apartment, he was offered probation before judgment. In legal parlance, that meant he could plead guilty without admitting guilt, a veritable slap on the wrist.

Unreal!

But it wasn't just the disposition of the case or the commissioner's tirade that stuck with me. It wasn't even the fact that working for the governor meant de facto immunity from the laws that apparently apply to the rest of us.

What still remains etched in my memory from that case is what the man said in court. The words he uttered before the plea bargain that stunned me, and I think more than anything encapsulates the true futility of the war on drugs:

"I don't have any animosity towards Detective Tabeling," he said before the verdict. "He was only doing his job."

Really? Only doing my job?

Did I actually need forgiveness? He was the one breaking the law, but apparently I was the one who committed the unforgivable sin of applying it equally.

To this day I still can't believe it — the arrogance.

Maybe it was haughtiness born of experience. Maybe it was because he was of the new growing class of untouchables, government officials turned drug dealers.

I mean, the guy got less than a slap on the wrist, especially given the sensitive nature of his job. A job for which one would think he would have been held to a higher standard. But he wasn't, he was in fact protected, shielded from the same laws that have sent millions to jail for crimes far less egregious.

And what's more, the perp got to keep his job. I'm not kidding.

But it was this case, and all the behind-the-scenes controversy, that stayed with me.

And it was the fear of this two-tiered level of justice forged in the prosecution of the drug war that prompted me to say Yes when an opportunity to get even deeper into it arose.

I guess in the back of my mind, I was hoping I could work to construct a better sense of how the drug business was growing. It was an opportunity to employ a big-picture strategy that I hoped would lead to better investigations and more productive arrests.

And less political interference.

Several months after my run-in with the governor's drug dealing staffer, I was called into the colonel's office, the same commander who had hung me out to dry when the commissioner chewed me out regarding the arrest.

"The State's Attorney's Office is forming a new Narcotics Strike Force, they have federal money to fund it. We're thinking of detailing you to run the whole thing," he told me.

"You'll work out of their offices, in the employ of the city state's attorney" — who at that juncture was Milton Allen — he said, adding: "Of course you will still work for me and report to me every morning and will be under my direction."

And then the esteemed colonel leaned over his desk and looked me straight in the eye.

"Now let me give you some advice: I don't always trust the State's Attorney's Office. So when you take the new position, I want you to report back to me on everything that happens in the office. Even if you have to go through people's desks and papers, I want to know everything that goes on."

I was caught totally off guard. First, by the opportunity, and then by the colonel's suggestion that I become a snitch.

"Look Colonel, I'm loyal to the department," I replied. "I would certainly tell you if I thought something was going on that would hurt us, but you have the wrong person if you want someone to look through people's desks."

The colonel smiled, but didn't utter another word.

Maybe he was testing me, or maybe the colonel wanted to get rid of me, or just didn't care if I was a stooge or not. I don't really know what he was thinking or why he didn't find someone else. Because a few months later I was sitting in an office in the old Mitchell Courthouse heading up a unit where I would learn once and for all everything I needed to know about the war on drugs.

And then some.

IT'S NOT HOW YOU START

The Baltimore Narcotics Strike Force was launched with a tiny bit of fanfare, and a very large number of public promises.

On my first day of work, then-State's Attorney Milton Allen held a press conference with Commissioner Pomerleau at the courthouse touting it as the answer to the increasingly violent and disruptive drug business. He said (and I'm paraphrasing here) that by employing experts in narcotics policing and drug-trade prosecution the unit would be able to handle complex investigations.

But the question he failed to address that day, a question which would loom over everything I did with that unit, was, Could we handle the politics of the drug business? Because even as the assembled dignitaries gushed over the idea of a special task force, in the back of my mind I was already troubled by my conversation with the colonel, and its implications for the operation itself.

If the drug business was entwined within the city's power structure, how could we investigate freely without stumbling onto another untouchable? Would we truly be insulated from interference if we caught another high profile dealer? And given the growing influence of the drug trade, wasn't that in fact inevitable?

Still, I couldn't help but be excited. Here was an assignment which required more than rounding up petty drug dealers. My mission, as communicated to me by Peter Ward, one of the best prosecutors working then for State's Attorney Allen, was to gather real intelligence about how the drug trade actually worked. To seek out and expose the major kingpins and organized muscle. And then I was expected to use that information to launch broad and substantive criminal investigations. To me, it was the best opportunity in the history of Baltimore law enforcement to make a dent in the city's drug trade, a truly exceptional forward-thinking strategy.

And at least at the onset, everything did seem to run smoothly.

One of the first things we did was to set up an infrastructure to gather intelligence. We wanted a clear picture of just how big the drug business was and who was running it. To achieve this goal, we used two tools: the community, and patrol officers.

We launched a 24-hour telephone hotline called BAN — Baltimore Against Narcotics — where anyone could leave an anonymous tip about drug dealing. And we publicized the number with the launch of the task force.

We also began gathering reports and coordinating tips and information from all the police districts across the city. Any calls regarding dealing or drug related crimes ended up in our office. The idea was to use big-picture information to inform the street-level strategy towards making meaningful arrests, not just lots of them.

I mean, up until the task force was organized our approach to drug enforcement had been ad hoc. Yes, we had been making lots of arrests, but we weren't learning anything from them. But now we were equipped to remedy that. It was the first time a single unit had been responsible for collating data and intelligence city-wide.

And the early results were encouraging. "Secret Lawman's Group Cracks Dope Cases, Compiles Key Data," the headline read in the *Baltimore News American* newspaper shortly after we got started.

The article recounted some of our successes, including bringing down a $2 million gambling operation, major arrests in a kidnapping and extortion ring, the disruption of a truck hijacking cartel that had stolen millions of dollars worth of vehicles, and an untold number of major drug busts.

We also took down Julius Salisbury, the self-acknowledged king-pin of the city's illegal gambling business.

Not bad, but also proof that effective law enforcement is not always about personnel or tactics, but communication. Taking on the illicit narcotics business citywide had led us to all the corruption and chaos that surrounds it. It was the big-picture strategy coupled with collaboration, that was netting big results.

But along with initial success, our first major problem cropped up. After the *News American* article appeared, I noticed a drop-off in intelligence from the districts. It was so extreme I had a hunch it was the byproduct of ill intent. And sure enough, not long after, I was tipped off that a lieutenant working at the Police Academy was telling officers and cadets not to funnel information to our squad.

I discussed it with Peter Ward and we launched an investigation through the Inspectional Services Division. And the report turned out to be true.

A witness told us the lieutenant in charge of the Criminal Investigations Division had been spreading the word to all who would listen, to stop cooperating with the task force. Our informant said that his message to the troops was simple: the task force was harming the police department, so don't tell us anything.

And thus we had the first salvo, the opening shot across the bow in what would become an internal agency-wide battle to shut us down.

I confronted the lieutenant at the academy, an encounter that didn't go well. He was, to say the least, defiant. I told him point-blank he had to stop.

His answer?

An unambiguous "Go fuck yourself!"

He actually admitted he'd been actively working against us. His reason, just as the witness said, was that we were taking big investigations away from the department. It was simply a turf war. In the end, he dared me to do anything about it.

"Do whatever you want," he said to me in the hallway of the Police Academy. "Take your best shot. You don't have the people behind you that are behind me."

And that was it; he continued working against us. But it didn't stop the task force, not at all.

We received nearly 4,000 tips through the hotline. Plenty of solid leads that led to multiple investigations and dozens of arrests. I was writing search warrants almost daily to execute raids in districts throughout the city. We had gathered so much intelligence that Milton Allen was preparing to impanel a grand jury that would hear testimony from a variety of witnesses.

It was a big deal; we created a list of over 100 people to subpoena. These were drug dealers, addicts, business owners; people from the so-called "all walks of life."

And if a witness failed to comply? A person who thought they could flout the law? Peter Ward made it clear in a follow-up newspaper interview that anyone who didn't show up would be held in contempt of court. Meaning that if you didn't obey the subpoena, you'd end up in jail.

It was one of the most exciting assignments of my career. We were starting to paint a picture of just how expansive the drug trade was. I had compiled a long list of potential drug operations in all sectors of the city.

We had a list, for example, of so-called baggers, 12 people who moved from one organization to another cutting and bagging heroin on a freelance basis. An elite group of cutters whose unique skill-set was in high demand. In fact, the 12 people we identified shuttled from one drug operation to another like high-priced consultants.

We had also traced cocaine suppliers back to New York City, including one big supplier who owned a sporting goods store in Brooklyn. Another man we tracked back to the Bronx was bringing 10 ounces of heroin a week into the city.

And then there were the family organizations, retail drug operations run out of barber shops, liquor stores, bowling alleys. We also uncovered a drug organization run by the director of

Baltimore's Model Cities Program, a group that operated out of an upscale social club, dealing heroin and cocaine.

We found a connection between a well known drug dealer named Big Head Brother and one of the city's most prominent and influential bail bondsmen turned state delegate named Turk Scott. An alliance that would surface later when Scott was indicted for bringing kilos of heroin from New York into Baltimore, and then was shot dead in the parking garage of Sutton Place Apartments by the vigilante group Black October, as I recounted in the previous chapter.

We received intelligence that a group named The Golden Spoon Club was also moving heroin into the city. We referred 634 tips to district detectives which led to 177 arrests.

We also learned that Frank Matthews, a major dealer of heroin to East Coast cities, was the primary supplier to our city. His contact in Baltimore was also Big Head Brother. But we also observed Matthews in the company of the wife of notorious drug dealer "Little Melvin" Williams, who later played The Deacon on "The Wire" television show.

Matthews, known as "The Black Caesar," remains one of the most mysterious figures in the history of the illicit drug trade. He was indeed one of the biggest dope dealers in the country, moving hundreds of kilos of drugs per month through a sophisticated East Coast network. But shortly after he organized a now legendary "Drug Summit" in Atlanta for African-American and Hispanic dealers, he was arrested in Las Vegas on drug charges after allegedly dropping $170,000 in a single night of gambling.

Matthews made bail, but soon disappeared. Despite a massive manhunt and an FBI bounty on his head, he simply vanished and has never been seen or heard from again.

However all this work was about to be short-circuited, laid to waste. But not because we ran out of money or leads, or couldn't handle the workload. And it was also not because I and the other officers in the task force couldn't work with prosecutors or were unable to develop promising cases. Instead, the entire operation was scuttled due to the decision of two Baltimore police officers to steal 1,250 bags of heroin.

What I mean is, it wasn't the overwhelming and pervasive drug trade that put us out of business. It was corruption from within.

It all started on a typical day in the fall of 1973. I was slated to visit Calvert Hall College High School to speak to students about the dangers of illicit drugs, an appointment I kept. But when I returned to the office, my secretary was red-faced.

"Lieutenant, you better run and hide," she said. "The state's attorney issued a summons for all the evidence from a case of missing drugs from evidence — the department's property division — and he's issued a subpoena for the police commissioner to appear before the grand jury."

But that wasn't all.

"There's a sergeant who's been trying to get in touch with you all morning."

I was stunned. It was the first I'd heard of it. I had a million questions and very few answers.

"Why do they want the commissioner to testify in front of the grand jury?" I asked.

"Something about some officers and missing drugs," she replied.

Unbelievable.

Officers absconding with drugs was unfortunately unremarkable. But the commissioner hauled in front of a grand jury? That was something entirely different.

Just to put this into context, it's pretty rare for the city's top prosecutor and top cop to spar in court. A war of words?... maybe. Famously, former Police Commissioner Ed Norris and ex-State's Attorney Patricia Jessamy battled it out in the press over a variety of issues. Most notably the failure of Jessamy to prosecute thousands of "zero tolerance" arrests, a policy discussed in Chapter 1, which used aggressive targeting of minor crimes that later led to hundreds of thousands of illegal incarcerations. But the war of words rarely if ever turned into a subpoena to appear before a grand jury. In fact, I don't know if it has ever happened before or since in the City of Baltimore.

Still, before I could figure out what was going on, the sergeant showed up with an envelope. He was someone I knew, a cop I respected. But he was a little jumpy when he handed me the letter. He couldn't look me in the eye.

"Steve, this is from the colonel."

"What's it about?"

"I don't know," he replied.

But of course he did. And it was a stunner. I was being transferred... immediately. My tenure at the Narcotics Strike Force was over, done, finished without an explanation.

The letter said I was to report immediately to something called the Crime Watch Unit. Eventually I would be transferred to the Northeastern District. Truthfully I'd never heard of the unit. So after I finished reading the colonel's letter, I took a long hard look at the sergeant.

"What is it, Steve?" he asked.

"You mean to tell me you didn't know this is an immediate transfer for me?"

"No I didn't."

But he was lying, he was the colonel's bagman. And bagmen always know what's inside the bag, so to speak.

Just as I was about to engage the sergeant in more pointed conversation about the orders, the phone rang with even more bad news. It was Tom Coppinger, another investigator from the police department working for the task force.

"Steve, you're not going to believe this — I just got an immediate transfer."

"Me too," I replied.

We were being dismantled from the inside. And worse, I didn't really understand why.

I mean, we were making progress. A special grand jury was impaneled and prepared to hear testimony, and now this? A transfer?

Still, I didn't have a choice. A police department is a paramilitary organization; you can't just ignore legal orders.

So I gathered up my belongings, put on a uniform and reported to the office of the chief of patrol where this so-called Crime Watch Unit was allegedly based.

I have to admit it was a difficult moment for me, the best job of my entire career sinking into a pool of political quicksand.

The last thing I wanted to do was leave that cramped office in the corner of the Mitchell Courthouse. To abandon some of the most substantive work I'd ever been involved in. Worst of all, it was the first time in my career I thought we had a real chance of making a dent in the drug business.

But that's what I did, that's what cops do.

We follow orders.

THE COMMISSIONER TURNS RED

They didn't have a desk for me when I arrived. In fact, my first meeting with the chief made it pretty clear my assignment had little to do with the so-called career development cited in the press.

"I have an order that you are not to talk to anyone," the chief of patrol said. "You're not to talk to the press, and if anyone makes any inquiries about this program you are not to comment."

And that was it. I was left high and dry in a closet. My work for the task force taming the city's drug business, exchanged for punching a time clock and staring out a window.

And as I sat in exile at Police Headquarters, the real story of how I ended up in administrative purgatory began to unfold.

Turns out 1,250 bags of heroin had indeed gone missing from Police Headquarters, key evidence in a case against a mid-level drug dealer named Robert Crawley. The narcotics were confiscated during a raid that netted $100,000 worth of drugs. It was evidence used to obtain a guilty verdict against Crawley at the conclusion of a three-day trial.

But despite a request from State's Attorney Allen, the police department had failed to explain how the drugs disappeared. Instead the department suspended two cops who were believed to be connected but not yet accused of stealing the drugs.

And that's why Allen decided that Pomerleau would have to answer to a grand jury.

Milton Allen, along with prosecutors like Pete Ward, didn't shrink from holding the police department accountable. In fact, they had a healthy sense of skepticism when it came to working with the cops. And who can blame them, when a couple pounds of heroin walks out the door of Headquarters?

I understand that the relationship between the State's Attorney's Office and the police department has been a hotly debated topic. Much has been made about friction between the two agencies. The underlying premise seems to be that both the police department and the State's Attorney's Office must get along to be effective. And that's partly true.

But you have to remember that prosecutors are also obligated to hold cops accountable. Police have unique arrest powers and unmatched investigative resources. Someone has to watch us and check our work. And that's the job of the state's attorney, a job Milton Allen and others in his office took seriously.

Which is why Allen subpoenaed Pomerleau. If cops did indeed steal the heroin out of evidence, then the thrust of our mission to dismantle the drug business was simply a sham. How could any agency effectively prosecute the drug business if it's also corrupted by it? And if cops were stealing drugs, and no one was held accountable, then we were for all intents and purposes in the drug business ourselves.

Knowing Pomerleau, I'm sure he was being less than cooperative with Allen. I'm positive he didn't want Allen meddling in an investigation that could potentially turn scandalous. My take is that the commissioner wanted to handle this potentially embarrassing incident internally. I mean, we had allegations two cops hauled a heck of a lot of heroin out of evidence control; not a pretty picture. And remember, Pomerleau was a control freak who prided himself on being an effective and ruthless administrator. So I'm more than sure he gave Allen a hard time every step of the way, because his reputation was on the line.

But the truth is, Allen was in the driver's seat. It was *his* decision how the investigation should proceed. Ultimately Allen would have to make the final call. And that was a good thing.

Think about it, the fact that such a large amount of heroin could be walked right out of Police Headquarters was certainly not a ringing endorsement of our integrity. This was big-time weight, a hell of a lot of drugs gone missing jeopardizing a pretty substantial case. If the cops who stole it weren't charged, then the criminal justice system in Baltimore was de facto corrupt.

So Allen had to do something, and unfortunately I was caught in the middle.

Soon I was a pawn in an ongoing feud played out in print over the future of the task force. A battle which started when Allen publicly characterized my transfer as retribution for his subpoena.

"In the absence of information from the police department," he said in a written statement released to the press, "I am forced to conclude that the transfer of these two fine officers resulted from the initiation by this office of a special grand jury investigation into the missing heroin case." And in that statement, a key and astounding fact: the police department had told Allen they suspected no criminal involvement in the disappearance of the drugs. Which is probably why Allen concluded his press release with this promise: "I deemed it my responsibility to the people of Baltimore to institute an investigation of the missing heroin."

Pomerleau's tepid response, also published in the *News American*, characterized the case as "sensitive," not criminal.

Meanwhile the press was doing a better job at uncovering the facts about the missing drugs than either agency.

The *News American* reported that a man named Joseph Perry was shot to death outside a bar on the 1400 block of Mount Street shortly after a deal to buy the missing drugs from crooked cops fell through. The dead man had apparently arranged a deal to move the drugs to a second buyer who either backed out or didn't come up with the cash.

The newspaper also revealed several high ranking cops had actively sought to keep the fact that drugs were missing quiet. The paper reported a police colonel had ordered a subordinate to "keep his mouth shut" about the missing evidence, apparently all to avoid the scandal which was now unfolding.

But the strategy didn't work. Not even close.

When newspaper headlines are screaming "Cover-up on Heroin Charged" it's pretty obvious efforts to keep things under wraps aren't panning out. And to make matters worse for Pomerleau, Allen was making headway in his own investigation.

Turns out the dead drug dealer Perry was also a close associate of

Little Melvin, with a pretty violent reputation. Perry had previously been arrested in 1963 for storming into a Mount Street bar waving a machine gun over his head at a crowd of patrons. His motivation, allegedly another botched narcotics deal. So Allen was starting to assemble evidence that made it clear cops not only stole the drugs, but had ties to some of the city's most notorious drug kingpins.

Meanwhile my name kept popping up in the paper.

In a follow-up article in the *News American* on the botched deal for the stolen heroin, a reporter recounted the dramatic march of four prosecutors from the Mitchell Courthouse to Pomerleau's office to serve subpoenas for evidence tied to the missing drugs. It was a taut retelling of a confrontation between the city's top two law enforcement agencies. As the same prosecutors were leaving with boxes of documents in hand, one of them overheard a senior commander cursing me for negligence.

"Tabeling should have told us about this," an unnamed source revealed in the article. "Why the hell didn't he tell us?"

Another commander quoted in the same story called me a traitor: "Tabeling seems to have forgotten where his loyalty was."

But I had supporters too, ironically enough, in the State's Attorney's Office. A group of 31 prosecutors wrote a letter to Pomerleau requesting my return. Peter Ward used his withering sense of British wit to dress down the commissioner's intransigence:

"It is an act not worthy of a man who is a commissioner of a police force of 3,500 men in a city with 900,000 persons," he opined to the *News American* regarding Pomerleau's decision to break up the task force by reassigning me and Lieutenant Coppinger.

As the investigation continued, I again found myself sitting in Pomerleau's office to answer for my lack of loyalty to the department. The commissioner simply couldn't forgive me for not tipping him off that Allen had been planning to subpoena him.

And again, he was spitting mad, spewing another expletive-filled tirade about my alleged antipathy towards the department. How a simple phone call could have prevented the whole unholy humiliation of a subpoena. He was his usual unrelenting self. Like the aforementioned pit bull, but now on steroids.

"I was at Calvert Hall, "I explained. "I didn't know about the subpoenas until I got back to the office."

And then I said something that maybe I shouldn't have.

"But even if I did know about them, I couldn't have told you because it would have been obstruction of justice. The law is pretty clear on that."

Now throughout this book I've emphasized respect for the law. I've tried to make the argument that the law is not a constraint as it is often portrayed, but an excellent tool for conducting effective investigations. But in this case, I should have kept my admiration for it to myself. Because Pomerleau unleashed a tirade that was notable in its fury even for him. Not just because of his surprisingly venomous take on all my faults and allegedly abject betrayal of the department, but because this time I really thought the guy was going to hit me. He seemed barely able to restrain himself from leaping over his desk and wringing my neck.

He turned so red, I thought he was going to erupt or have a stroke. It was an even bet.

Finally, after he calmed down, he just sat in his chair and stared at me. Then he uttered a sentence which caught me completely off-guard.

"I'm sending you back to that office until the investigation is finished."

I was completely shocked. After all the yelling and screaming, and now another transfer? Now I was going back?

Again, I spoke without thinking.

"Sir, I don't want to go back. I'm happy being back in uniform."

Again, a bad idea. Because within seconds of the words leaving my mouth, he stood up and pounded his fist on the desk.

"Listen to me! goddamn you! You don't have any choice. You're going to go where I tell you to go, you're going to like it, and I don't want to hear any more from you about it," he yelled.

"Now get the hell out of my office!"

BACK IN THE DOGHOUSE

And that was it, another drubbing to punctuate my illustrious career.

I was frankly depressed. Walking back to my non-office to once again pick up my things, I remembered advice given to me when I was a rookie fresh out of the academy that at the moment seemed remarkably prescient.

"Nobody ever got ahead in this department by working," an aging veteran cop had told me. "To succeed, you need to make friends with a politician."

True enough.

When I arrived back at the task force offices, there was another surprise waiting in the form of a cop. A lieutenant who I knew, standing next to my desk staring at his shoes.

"I feel bad about this," he explained. "I've been ordered to watch you, and go through your desk and others and report back to the commissioner's office so we don't get blindsided again."

What a shock. First I was transferred back into the unit, and now I'm under surveillance. At least the lieutenant seemed refreshingly ambivalent about his assignment.

"I'm not going to do it. I'm not searching anyone's desk," he said evenly. "I'm not going after other cops or doing their dirty work."

So I stayed with the unit until the investigation into the missing drugs was concluded, but my work for all intents and purposes was finished. The best laid plans of commissioners and cops had indeed gone for naught.

We'd lost momentum, and frankly I had lost interest. The whole ordeal was an exemplar of the futility of trying to dismantle the drug business through enforcement. The politics, money, and allure of illicit narcotics was too appealing. Cops couldn't fight the human predilection for screwing with the mind, at least not with guns and badges. The drug business in the city was so entrenched there was little we could do without touching someone politically connected or legally untouchable.

The two aforementioned cops were charged with stealing the dope. The arrest of a man named Horace Hannah who had 200 bags of heroin in his possession proved to be their undoing.

The small time drug dealer got caught with the bags from the same stash, and admitted to investigators the dope came from evidence. The officers were tried, one of whom was convicted and ultimately sentenced to three years in prison. It was a major scandal with unintended fallout, taking down our best chance, the task force, to fix the root cause of the problem.

As for me, I asked for, and received a transfer to the city's vaunted Homicide Unit. It was a bittersweet moment. I was proud of our work, but troubled and haunted by the aftermath and how it was so easily foiled from within.

Who knows what we could have done had two cops not stolen a pile of heroin from the department's property division? Who can fathom what that special grand jury would have uncovered had it not been caught in the crosshairs of a dispute between the police commissioner and the city's top prosecutor? What might have happened had we been able to continue our quest for the truth about the drug business in Baltimore? Would that unvarnished, unapologetic dose of reality have altered the city's path as it descended into a long decline fueled by the violence and disruption of the drug trade?

I think so.

It makes you wonder about this ongoing business of eradicating drugs that seems to continue unabated. It's like we're cycling through the same problems and issues over and over without learning anything. Instead, we now use even more brutal and constitutionally suspect tactics to prosecute this war called "run and gun," hitting the drug corners with brute force and making quick and dirty arrests.

The war rages on even as the public is starting to push back. Voters in Colorado and Washington are scaling back drug laws by approving referenda which legalize recreational use of marijuana. Partly because they realize amid all this so-called warring, the price of illicit drugs like cocaine and heroin has gotten cheaper, and the supply even more abundant. But mostly because they understand addiction is a health problem, not a prison problem.

The people understand it's futile, so why can't the cops?

I mean, what are we really trying to achieve? What's the goal? Is it to destroy neighborhoods, or to grow them? Is it to criminalize addicts or to cure them? Is it to incarcerate the poor while the rich continue to indulge?

Whatever the goal, it seems clear we've lost sight of it now. Instead, we have a multi-billion-dollar drug-warring bureaucracy which is self-preserving and socially destructive, an unrelenting strategy of mindless interdiction that has warped policing from the inside.

That's why I return occasionally to the neighborhood of my youth. Not because the ruins are a self-affirming testament to the misbegotten war on drugs. Or to convince myself that better, more effective policing could have kept my neighborhood intact.

No, I return so I can remember why it's important to recount history even when it's a story of abject failure. To remind myself it's just as important to reveal the truth about our mistakes as it is to tell tales of triumph.

Take the word of an old man who has been a cop for six decades, that this war cannot be won. Bear in mind these are the thoughts of an officer who has witnessed both tangible results and the destructive aftermath of turning police against the community to fight a battle for which we are not equipped.

And if you disagree with me and still think we're on the right path, join me for a walk here. Take a firsthand look at the results. Witness the aftermath of a war sold to us as a cure for an insatiable human desire. A fight we are told we're losing because there just aren't enough cops to win it.

You'll see, from wandering through a back alley dotted with hollowed-out row homes, my disconsolate neighborhood is too far gone to fix with cops and courts. As we pass through the broken city, this land of vacants, you'll confront firsthand the desolate truths of a story untold: The tale of how a once vibrant, thriving neighborhood turned to dust.

Not because we weren't safe. But because of a war that will never end.

CHAPTER SEVEN:
SPEAKER FOR THE DEAD

How To Solve a Murder
Without a Body

YOU CAN'T STOP MURDER

Who speaks for the dead? Who advocates for the victim snatched from the earth by the hands of another?

Who is willing to stand up for the murdered and tell their stories? To remember how they lived, and tell the truth about their demise.

Who is responsible for writing the final chapter of their time on earth, especially when it ends violently? And most important, who ensures the crime of taking their life does not go unpunished?

Sometimes that job falls squarely on the shoulders of a cop. In fact, it is too often solely the task of cops.

More victims than I care to remember die alone. Not in solitary per se, but amid the isolation born of indiscriminate violence and social decay in an impoverished city. Paupers in paupers' graves with no one to speak on their behalf.

So the ugly truth is, sometimes all they have is us: cops.

But the dead need witnesses, too. They need people who will stand up and tell their stories. Speakers who don't have guns or wear badges. The often unacknowledged few who dare to speak for the departed. Those who without incentive or benefit, and sometimes under threat of death, tell the tales of the dead in order to bring justice to the living.

Speakers for the murdered who display a level of courage that is as rare and awe-inspiring as it is also difficult to explain. It's the type of courage only a homicide detective is familiar with: the bearer of witness to a killing, the accuser of last resort of the most violent among us.

That's because the murder witness, the crucial marrow of a criminal case, takes risks more daunting than any cop. Yet while they play this critical role in cases against the most dangerous criminals, there is little interest in the witnesses' long-term well-being. The grave risks they take in court yield little in material or moral support once the case is finished.

The State's Attorney's Office for Baltimore City has spent on average just $500,000 annually for witness protection over the past decade — funds which offer scant protection to citizens who testify. And in most cases, these brave souls are left on their own to survive in the city's most violent neighborhoods.

Take the recent murder trial of a Bloods gang member named Elliot Wilkes, a/k/a "Shitty."

I remember it solely because of a witness. A witness whose bravery exemplifies the risks people take to witness for the dead. It was one of dozens of under-the-radar murder trials that proceed with little fanfare in Baltimore courtrooms.

Wilkes was accused of shooting a man after his 10-year-old cousin got into a fight with the victim's sibling. The killing occurred after Wilkes received a call from his younger relative describing the altercation, prompting Wilkes and the boy to drive to the scene to confront several young men who lived in the neighborhood where the fight occurred. Shortly after they arrived a confrontation ensued and shots were fired. Left for dead was the uncle of the boy who beat up Wilkes' cousin.

But a woman witnessed parts of the incident. And from her account, homicide detectives built a case against Wilkes and charged him with murder. What happened during the trial proves my point about the moral dilemma of people who choose to speak for the dead in Baltimore.

Sit and observe a murder trial in Baltimore. It won't take long to figure out the social geography of the courtroom. The defendant's family and friends usually sit on one side facing the judge, directly behind the defense table. On the opposite side, the victim's relatives line up behind the prosecutor.

It's a clear and well-defined parsing of partisans that can lead to tensions, particularly after a verdict. In fact, post-trial rancor can turn violent, which is why sheriff's deputies line the courtroom shortly before a contentious verdict.

But during this particular trial there was not a single person on the side of the victim. The only people who attended all the proceedings were roughly a dozen young men, possibly gang members, sitting directly behind Wilkes, glaring at the jury.

The witness was a young woman, a single mother with a part-time job living in one of the most dangerous neighborhoods in the country. You know the type, the unwed mother raising a couple of kids. The beleaguered near-teen who is often demonized as the root cause of the city's ongoing ills. But as I sat there and watched her give witness to the death of a man who had not a single relative in the courtroom, I realized she was in fact one of the bravest women in Baltimore.

Sitting on the witness stand roughly 10 feet removed from a posse of Wilkes' friends, she recounted a version of events that squarely put the blame on Wilkes. Without a single ally or friend in that courtroom other than the prosecutor, she concisely and defiantly told the tale of Wilkes' alleged crime. Even as the probable gang members stared her down and the defense attorney attempted to pick apart her story, she refused to budge.

Unfortunately for her, however, Wilkes was acquitted. Maybe the jury was intimidated by the hostile stares from the assembly of suspected Bloods, or perhaps he was simply innocent. Who knows?

But one can only imagine the consequences for her. After testifying against Wilkes, she was more than likely left to fend for herself. A young woman without means stuck living around the corner from Wilkes, her life and his conjoined by a failed murder prosecution.

That case, and the dilemma faced by the young woman who testified, show another side of the story of homicide in Baltimore: how we often forget or ignore that amid the chaos there is a tremendous and unrelenting human thirst for justice. And that quite often in the communities we revile or blame for seemingly unmitigated dysfunction, there are people willing to risk their lives to make things better.

In fact, there was another case I worked where one of the most unlikely speakers chose to be heard. A brave young girl who refused to let her brother's death go unnoticed. A child whose quest to avenge her younger sibling's untimely demise made her one of the bravest witnesses I'd ever known.

And it all started with a whisper from a gurney.

"Michael is dead."

"Who is Michael?" asked an officer.

"My brother."

Those were words uttered by a 10-year-old girl in the emergency room of Johns Hopkins Hospital in May of 1974, a little kid with a grave injury who was speaking on behalf of the dead — her five-year-old brother Michael.

She had appeared out of thin air, a skinny, emaciated kid with a grisly wound to her left buttock. An injured child who walked into the Monument Street emergency room at Johns Hopkins and presented herself to the nurse on duty, a chunk of her backside missing, a piece of flesh hacked away like gristle.

She trembled with fear as the doctor examined it, but remained tight-lipped on how it happened.

But when the doctor called police, the girl who was unwilling to answer questions about her own injury did indeed have something to say. She leaned over the gurney to whisper in the officer's ear, fearful but determined.

And then she said it, the words which would launch one of the most troubling and bizarre investigations of my career.

"Michael is dead."

It was a cryptic revelation. A child who wanted someone to know, a shy little girl seeking a sympathetic ear to hear her plea for the deceased.

She was the speaker for the death of Michael, determined to ensure his passing wouldn't go unnoticed.

Because, indeed, without her testimony, it most likely would have.

It's possible no one would have noticed the disappearance of a quiet, unassuming five-year-old. A boy whose neighbors said he looked emaciated. An awkward child whose teachers told us walked with a limp. A small, skinny kid occasionally tossed like a bag of garbage onto a metal porch, who might indeed have slipped into the abyss, unseen.

He might have simply slipped away, just another neglected child living on the East Side of Baltimore, gone and forgotten.

But not this time, because his sister wouldn't allow it. She was willing to speak on the death of her brother.

And the words she said to the cop while lying in the emergency room set in motion a series of events that would culminate in one of the strangest, most troubling cases I ever worked. A case which reaffirmed the old police axiom: the worst cruelty is reserved for children. But it also served as an example of a larger truism:

You can't stop murder, but sometimes you can solve it.

Forgive me, you have to solve it — no, you *must* solve it.

Still, this is an unspoken cop's oath we often forget. This happens because it's so easy to forget. In the clamor to book arrests, make stats, and earn our overtime, we frequently forget the dead. The dead don't complain and even their families can soon become easy to ignore.

You don't believe me? On television, murders are solved at a rarified rate. The determined detective, the equally committed prosecutor, the high-tech investigation, and the case neatly wrapped up by the time the last commercial is played.

But the real numbers tell a different story.

In 2012 — and I'm not sure of the exact date — the U.S. passed a grim milestone: 200,000 unsolved murders. Open homicide cases stretching back to 1980 that for one reason or another have not resulted in an arrest.

It's a breathtaking number. Two-hundred-thousand slayings unavenged, thousands of murderers who remain unpunished. Killers who walk the streets, free to roam among the innocent, near-certain their crimes will remain secret.

And that annoys the hell out of me.

To be an effective homicide detective, murder has to irk you, it has to make you angry.

I'm not talking about street vengeance. Or the instinctual rage that occurs when someone you love is threatened. What I mean is, you need a steady sense of indignation, an attitude. A psychic intolerance for the act itself, a real disdain for the arrogance of the murderer, the person who made the decision to kill, because that person didn't think you'd catch him.

Without it, you might not have the wherewithal to solve the cases. The type of dedication to work consecutive 24-hour days without sleep like we did for half a week following the City Hall shooting. And then get up and do it again another two days later when an 18-year-old picks up a gun and starts shooting cops.

You have to become a speaker for the dead. You have to bear stubborn witness to the deaths of victims you never knew. You have to be persistent enough to ensure their stories get told. Tales of their last moments on earth, you turn into evidence, proof to ensure the psychopaths who brought about their demise are brought to justice.

But in the case of Michael, not only was the tale of his death a mystery, his body was nowhere to be found. He had vanished without a trace.

He was gone, and forgotten. Almost.

Of course, East Baltimore was in the early stages then of becoming a mortal swamp. The nascent and increasingly violent drug business was starting to suck up souls and toss bodies into vacant row homes and back alleys faster than we could find them.

But this victim was a child — a five-year-old boy.

His sister had given us a statement. Not much information other than that her brother had been vomiting one night, and then was gone the next morning. When she asked her mother where Michael was, the girl was simply told to shut up and mind her business.

But along with the few tidbits of information about the disappearance of Michael, was a more chilling tale of abuse.

She told us her stepfather was brutal. A burly, 250-pound man with an unhealthy temper.

He used to beat all the children, she said, but saved the worst for her younger brother. He would toss Michael headfirst onto a metal porch. He would use Michael's head to extinguish cigarette butts, as the man sat playing poker with his friends.

And that was just the lurid stuff she was willing to talk about.

But it was more than enough to justify a visit to the home where Michael lived with his sister and another brother.

So when we arrived at the home of Mary Alice Terry in May of 1974, I was hardly surprised by her answer when we asked to see Michael.

"He's with his aunt in North Carolina," she said.

The mother, Mrs. Terry, was friendly, not dismissive. She seemed remarkably at ease. Just composed enough that we could have accepted her explanation and been done with it, thanked her for her time and walked away without a second thought. There were more than enough murder cases on the board back at Homicide to keep us busy.

But I couldn't ignore Michael's sister. And I couldn't let the possibility of a brutal murder of a five-year-old child go unpunished. Besides, this woman was too calm. Not to mention the fact we were missing a crucial piece of evidence:

We didn't have a body.

That's right, the critical starting point for a homicide case, a corpse. I don't mean to sound callous, we're talking about a kid. But it's pretty hard to prove a murder if the body is nowhere to be found.

Hard, but not impossible.

We also asked Mrs. Terry about the injuries to her daughter, and again she calmly explained that the girl had fallen down the stairs. Still, the explanation didn't hold water, everything was just too cool. She was too poised, too self-possessed. As I used to tell young cops at the Police Academy, guilty people nearly always come off as calm.

I realize that on television the guilty people sweat, plead, and act shifty, while the innocent remain composed, unfazed, and, well,... innocent. But the opposite is true in real life, at least from my experience. The innocent are angry, indignant, and they let you know it.

The guilty are calm as a corpse.

Still, I didn't want to press Mrs. Terry too hard. Mainly, I didn't want her to know I was suspicious. We already knew that if Michael was in fact dead, she must have disposed of the body pretty effectively. Her son had died mysteriously; she got rid of his corpse, and was now acting like he was on vacation.

Pretty hardcore behavior for a housewife. So I didn't want to give her any inkling that I would be pursuing the case, lest she work harder to cover her tracks.

The first thing we did was some basic detective work: we asked around. We talked with neighbors, friends of the family, and teachers. And the picture they all painted was ugly.

The abuse of Michael was not a secret. As I mentioned, he walked with a limp, a hitch in his stride that was hard to miss. Neighbors also told us they frequently heard the boy crying as he was tossed out onto the porch like unwanted refuse.

But then the most unsettling evidence, witness accounts that made me even more determined to solve the case. Seriously, even in a city prone to cruelty, what happened to Michael was shocking.

According to the kids in the neighborhood, they would occasionally see Michael hanging upside down in the basement of his parents' home. That's right: they said he was hoisted by his ankles upside down.

His friends told us they were drawn to the window by his cries for help. The torture would last for hours, sometimes even a day. In fact, some of the boys told me they would push bread in between the bars because Michael would beg for food. It was bizarre, twisted and cruel, and even harder to understand as a father of a son myself.

Cruelty is natural, and Baltimore has its own particular brand of it. But even the savagery common among adults in this city pales in comparison to this. I don't know if it was a sign of things to come, a new level of depravity visited upon children, a forerunner of Baltimore's becoming the murder capital of the nation. But despite my years of experience dealing with all sorts of grisly murder, it unnerved me.

I know I've argued that a detective has to be equal in his application of effort for each and every killing. It's a sort of unwritten pact between the cop and the decedent. But if I were to be completely honest, this case was different. This case had to be solved. Body or not, we were putting this one down.

So I got in the car and headed to North Carolina.

If we couldn't find little Michael, we were going to pursue each and every lead to the bitter end. If his imperturbable mother said he was in Winston-Salem, we were going to check it out.

In person.

So I traveled to Winston with the prosecutor assigned to the case, Marianne Willin-Saar. We drove some eight hours, straight to the driveway of Michael's aunt's house.

The aunt was a quiet, pleasant woman, I think a bit stunned to see a cop and a prosecutor standing on her doorstep. But otherwise, she was simply perplexed.

"Ma'am," I said, "we're looking for Michael, your nephew."

"He used to live here," she told us. "But he moved to Baltimore. Is something wrong?"

I told her Michael was missing, though I didn't let on that his mother had said he was in North Carolina. She became distraught, so I spent the rest of the visit comforting her as best I could.

Back in Baltimore, a friend of Michael's stepfather had called Homicide. According to the detective who took the call, the friend wanted to talk.

When we arrived at his home, I could tell he was conflicted. He was sweating, nervous and jumpy. It was obvious he wanted to get something off his chest, but didn't want to snitch on his friend.

Still, the man talked, and he gave us plenty.

He said the first time he saw Michael enduring abuse was during a poker game. The boy's stepfather, Charles Terry, had put a cigarette out on the kid's head. He'd also seen Terry kick the kid viciously in the butt. But that wasn't all.

The next day after a game that had lingered well past midnight,

Mary Terry asked him to help move a laundry bag. It was too heavy for Charles to move by himself, she told him. And then she said something cryptic: "I don't want anyone to see it."

So they took the bag, loaded it into a car, and drove.

Charles directed him to the old Kaiser Aluminum plant in Baltimore County, a sprawling industrial complex where he had recently worked on a storm drain. And there, he told us, Charles simply stuffed the bag down one of the storm drains. That's right, the body of a five-year-old child unceremoniously dropped down a hole.

It was a big break for us. We now had a bead on the body. So I quickly assembled a few detectives and visited the site.

But it turned out the impromptu burial had occurred just before a huge rainstorm. When we arrived, a supervisor told us the drain had clogged during the storm. An industrial plumber was called, and the stoppage was forced through the drainage system and into the bay. It was an unpleasant moment to say the least when we realized what had more than likely caused the backup: Michael's body.

The child, unceremoniously buried, had simply vanished down a drain.

So that was it, the body was gone. Thanks to the quick thinking of a heartless mother and unwitting complicity of a family friend, Michael had vanished. Not a trace to be found. And with the luck of a serendipitous rainstorm, all evidence of the child's existence had been washed away.

But I still wasn't giving up. Someone needed to speak for this unfortunate dead child. And I was determined it was going to be his sister and me.

So I decided to meet with State Medical Examiner Dr. Hormerz Guard. I needed him to consider a proposition that had been percolating in my mind since the case began. I was thinking, maybe we could solve this case without a body. Maybe, with the right amount of circumstantial evidence and a creative medical examiner we could take this case to court.

I just needed Dr. Guard to declare Michael's death a homicide.

I told him about Michael, the circumstances surrounding his disappearance, and the eyewitness accounts of abuse we had gathered. I also shared with him the probability that the body would never be recovered, that we had information the corpse had been stuffed down a drain and more than likely lost in a flood of rainwater a few days before we were tipped off.

And I finally assured him that I believed wholeheartedly the child had been murdered. So when I asked him to declare Michael dead — and, more importantly, classify his death as a homicide — I wasn't sure if he would agree.

But Dr. Guard was receptive to my pleading, although cautious. He simply instructed me to share all the evidence with him and he'd do whatever he could to help.

"I'll do what I can," he told me.

It was all I could ask for. But I needed more.

I wanted to work on the mother; the stepfather was a dead-eyed monster. I figured Michael's mom might feel some guilt. I mean, it was her son, after all.

My strategy was to gather enough evidence to break her, to make her admit to her crime. So I decided to piece together a comprehensive narrative of just how Michael died. A blow by blow detailed account of her crime that would force her to confront it, and in the end, admit her guilt.

So we talked to everyone we could, including Michael's brother and sister, all of course under the pretense that we were still looking for Michael. From dozens of interviews and witness statements we pieced together a working narrative of Michael's final days on earth.

First we learned that the boy had been living with the aunt we visited in Winston until early November 1973. Later that month he moved to Baltimore to join his mother and her new husband. But shortly after he arrived, a cycle of vicious beatings punctuated with heinous torture began. And while his stepfather showed little personality or gumption under questioning, apparently behind closed doors he was an inventive monster.

He would beat Michael with a variety of blunt instruments, a white leather strap, a big white stick, a red leather strap, and a dog leash.

And his vicious aptitude wasn't limited to beatings.

There was the torturous butting-out of cigarettes on his head, and the upside-down hangings which his sister told us were so brutal that blood would drip on the floor as Michael twisted in a door frame, weeping softly.

Worse for Michael, his mother was in on it. His sister told us "she didn't feed him a lot." And when he asked for food, she'd toss him naked into the basement, which is where his friends found him begging for something to eat.

And it wasn't the stepfather who administered the vicious beatdown that left him with a limp. That extraordinary abuse was the work of his mother.

Truthfully, as the story unfolded, I was amazed the boy survived as long as he did. I mean, the regimen of torture inflicted upon this child would have been difficult even for a grown person to endure. In fact, it was so unrelentingly cruel, Michael was like a veritable prisoner of war.

It was also difficult for me to comprehend the complicity of his mother. I've investigated plenty of cases where men turned a brutal hand on family members, often with deadly consequences. As a cop gaining more experience of the innate brutality of Baltimore, I was used to men behaving badly. But this was different: a callous woman with complete disregard for the welfare of her children was relatively new to me.

Maybe it was a bad sign for the City of Baltimore. An inauspicious portent of the misery to come. I mean, when women lose their humanity all bets are off.

But back to events leading up to Michael's death.

We learned that Michael was bedridden for several days before he died. His brother and sister told us the stepfather had administered several notably vicious beatings, leaving Michael so weak he could barely move.

For several days he was constantly vomiting, too weak to get out of bed. The last time his sister saw Michael, he was lying naked on a mattress.

And then the reluctant family friend decided to divulge more details.

The friend confirmed it was Michael's mother who actually asked him to move the body. She led him upstairs and into a bedroom where Michael was lying face down, dead. His buttocks, the friend recalled, were scarred and bloodied.

"After Charles beat him he started throwing up," she told the friend. She convinced him to help her place the body in a laundry bag and toss it down the manhole.

And that was it. The next morning, after the storm, Michael was gone.

So now we had an eyewitness who had seen the corpse. Pretty good proof the child was dead. Plus a firsthand-witness account of Mary Alice Terry's despicable role in her son's murder.

Bottom line, I now knew everything — everything, that is, except why. Why did she do it? How did she summon the detachment to stuff her own son's remains into a laundry bag? Where did she find the perverse strength to hand Michael's tiny, emaciated body to a friend for an ignominious burial in a drain pipe?

The "why?" was the tough part, the "why."

So I decided to pay another visit to Mrs. Terry. My goal was to slowly but surely peel away the layers of her self-confidence by confronting her with evidence.

I needed to reach what I call a factual breaking point. The threshold where what I know is so overwhelming, the suspect realizes there's simply no benefit to lying. The tipping point where the only option left is to cut a deal, or blame somebody else.

And sure enough she did.

I told her point-blank what we knew. I recounted the abuse in excruciating detail. I even went step-by-step over the final days of Michael's life. I didn't soft-pedal or hold back. I told her the story with the steady tone of a man sitting in judgment. Not of her deeds, but her ability to lie in the face of undeniable truth.

And it worked.

I've seen it before, the diminution of a liar. I've watched the subtle signs of surprise flutter across the face of a killer as I roll out the facts. Particularly the eyes, which seem to grow dimmer as I reveal each irrefutable piece of the puzzle.

And just like many of the killers I had confronted before, the story I told Mary Alice Terry soon erased her confident, smug grin, her disingenuous poise quickly fading into a taut expression of increasing despair.

And then I played my trump card.

"He said you told him."

"Told him what?" she asked.

"That it was Michael's body in the bag. You said to Charles, 'We might as well tell him, he's going to find out anyway.'"

And that just about did it. She feigned surprise, then tried dismissive. But I kept up the pressure, knowing full well she was about to break.

"We know, and you know we know. It would be better for your conscience and for Michael if you just tell us the truth."

And then she did. And her story was actually unsurprising.

It wasn't her fault, she insisted. Seriously.

She was actually trying to protect Michael's siblings, she maintained. It was because the stepfather threatened to kill Michael's brother and sister if she told the cops. He was domineering and evil. She didn't have a choice.

She didn't have a choice? Her denial is still ringing in my ears.

But of course she did have a choice. No one had to die. I'm not saying her dilemma was easy, but murdering your own son? It's just too hard to understand, even, as I said before, in a town like Baltimore that manufactures tales of cruelty as by-products of communal dysfunction.

Still, with her confession we had a case. Shortly after she spilled the beans both mother and stepfather were indicted on charges of second degree murder and child abuse. I felt a bit of satisfaction, we'd brought charges without a body, no easy feat. But the hard part of this whole ordeal remained.

The trial.

Remember, charging is the relatively easy part; proving the charges to a jury beyond a reasonable doubt is much more difficult. Yes, we had some good witnesses, the family friend, teachers, neighbors. But the two key witnesses we wanted to put on the stand were children — kids no less. Michael's older brother and sister who would have to sit in the witness stand and literally tell the jury that their mother killed their younger sibling.

Not an easy thing to do, but as I said before, sometimes in the face of injustice the least likely stand up to the test.

Meanwhile, we had another vexing problem. Without a body the medical examiner had yet to rule Michael's death a homicide. So we devised a strategy.

Dr. Guard would sit in the courtroom and observe. He would listen to the witnesses and take note of their testimony. Then, as our final witness he would provide his opinion that Michael's death was indeed a homicide.

It seemed like a good plan, but I was still nervous. We had a strong case, but it relied on the testimony of children. A brother and sister tasked with putting their own mother away for decades. It was quite a burden for two innocent kids, to implicate their own mother. I don't care how cruel she was, or what she did to Michael, the person on trial was still their flesh and blood.

For whatever reason, the siblings felt comfortable with me. So during the trial I stayed with them at the old Emerson Hotel across the street from the courthouse. Every morning before court began we'd have breakfast together. It was a ritual that seemed to soothe them.

Perhaps it gave them a sense that somebody cared about them. Or maybe they just needed some sense of family, however odd, to get through the trial. It really was the least I could do. In a sense, I adopted them.

Still, the day they testified was a day I will never forget. Nothing could have prepared me for what happened.

As Michael's sister took the stand, I was indeed nervous. I worried like a father. My concern, not just what she would say but how the added stress of testifying against her mother would affect her? Forced to re-live the crime, would she suffer? Was it too much to ask a kid who had already been abused to recall events so horrifying?

But soon my fears evaporated. She told the story down to the last detail without wavering. She recounted all the horrible beatings, the torture, and finally the disappearance of her brother. And when the prosecutor asked her to point to the person in the courtroom who committed these heinous crimes, she remained calm. She raised her hand without hesitation and pointed right at her mother sitting at the defendant's table.

"She did it."

The courtroom was silent, the jurors rapt. There was not a person watching who was not transfixed. People simply gaped as the little 10-year-old girl pointed an accusatory finger at two adults sitting at the defendants' table, one of them her mother. A girl whose expression never changed or courage wavered. She just pointed — and continued to do so even after the prosecutor moved on to the next question.

And she pointed. And said it again without being asked.

"They did it."

And that was it, the case was over.

Yes, our last witness, the medical examiner, testified Michael died from child abuse. And yes, we had a half dozen other witnesses who detailed abuses by Michael's mother and stepfather.

But it wasn't needed, not one bit. A 10-year-old girl had won the case. Her extraordinary bravery, her fearless accusatory finger pointed across the courtroom as the jury sat spellbound was the only evidence we really needed. In a single gesture she had completed her quest to avenge Michael's death. In one enervating moment on the witness stand she proffered the only testimony that ultimately mattered.

I wasn't surprised when the jury came back with a guilty verdict. Second degree murder and child abuse, a conviction which would result in a sentence of 50 years for both so-called parents. It took the jurors just a few hours. The little girl had told them all they needed to know.

Guilty as charged.

I don't know what happened to those kids, or if they ever saw their mother again. Truthfully I wish I did. I wish I could find that brave young girl and shake her hand. See how her life turned out. Find out what she may have accomplished, and how she fared after the trauma of watching her brother die and her mother and stepfather go to prison.

But most all, I wish I could tell her kids and her loved ones how brave she was. How she stood up for an uncle or a cousin that they would never meet. How her refusal to let young Michael's death go unnoticed had probably saved her life and the life of her surviving brother. How she ensured that a cruel and terrible man and woman would never hurt another child.

I really wish I could somehow pay tribute to that child who became the true speaker for the dead. The truth teller who told the tale of a five-year-old child who died at the hands of his own mother, all the while living with two monsters who threatened to do the same to her.

A little girl who refused to remain silent. Who spoke up for her dead brother, without regard for her own safety or herself.

The bravest little girl I've ever met.

CHAPTER EIGHT:
TO VICE IS HUMAN;
TO ERR, POLICE

Gambling and Cops
on Pennsylvania Avenue

Take it from me, there's nothing more complicated, exhausting — and risky — than investigating other cops.

Imagine for a minute that your boss came to you with allegations that co-workers were breaking the law. Imagine if he or she then asked you to investigate their crimes and build a case against them.

Sure, it sounds intriguing, maybe even exciting to someone who has never done it.

But being the bad guy is not fun; in fact, if you're the cop going after other cops it can be downright dangerous.

One thing you learn quickly as an investigator is that no one wants to get caught. And if the suspects have a gun and a badge, they can sure enough make it harder for you to catch them.

And that's not even accounting for the well known fact that investigating cops is a quick path to occupational isolation and inevitable institutional blowback.

But that doesn't mean it's not important. In fact, in my opinion, as a society, how we police ourselves is a good indicator of how effective a police department will be in general.

That's because cops who don't follow the law aren't very good at enforcing it.

And therein lies the rub.

How do you police people who carry guns and badges? How is it possible to create an enforcement mechanism that can get past the insular relationships and tight-knit community of cops to fer-ret out the bad ones?

It's not easy, to say the least.

That's why when I read the statement in the downtown cham-bers of the Baltimore Criminal Justice Commission in the spring of 1966, I knew I was headed into a world of trouble.

Cop trouble, the kind that hits you across the forehead. A sense of foreboding that percolates in the mind, an instinctive sixth sense that makes you naturally wary of a potential career-ending mess.

And by the time I finished reading the statement of the woman who recounted how Baltimore City police officers were involved in the numbers racket, I knew the end result of the case before it even began.

Like I said: Trouble.

I had been called to the offices of the Criminal Justice Commission back then by one of the best legal minds in the city, now-retired Court of Special Appeals Judge Charles E. Moylan Jr.

Judge Moylan, who was then city state's attorney, had gathered several high ranking law enforcement officials there at the behest of a reporter from the *Baltimore Sun*. The reporter had apparently stumbled onto evidence that several city police officers were involved with a large numbers operation on Pennsylvania Avenue.

Evidence in the form of a witness.

When I arrived, I sat down to read the witness's statement in the company of Judge Moylan, Ralph Murdy, a former FBI agent who was head of the commission, interim Police Commissioner George Gelston, and an ambitious *Sun* reporter.

It was an odd group to say the least.

The witness told us about her knowledge of a relationship between a powerful cop and a suspected numbers man named Phil Taylor who worked an illegal lottery operation at 1500 Pennsylvania Avenue — home to a barbershop, hotel and eatery, and also, according to the witness, a sizable numbers business.

But it wasn't the tale of the gambling operation that gave me pause. No, it was something else, something that sparked the feeling of foreboding every cop develops over the course of his or her career.

Call it a survival instinct.

I think any police officer, particularly an investigator, will under-stand when I say that the longer you wear the uniform you either develop an extraordinary sense to sniff out trouble — or you soon find yourself working security in a parking garage. I'm not talking about the standard bad-guy-with-a-gun trouble. No, that comes the minute you put on the uniform.

I'm talking about the ability to see the shit before it hits the fan. The aforementioned sixth sense that tells you the situation you're wading into is going to get you into trouble that will require a crowbar to pry you out of.

It's like witnessing a car accident in slow motion, you see two vehicles on a collision course long before they arrive at the point of impact.

I know this sixth sense and I believe in it because when I was called to that meeting downtown in the Criminal Justice Commission's office, I recognized from the minute I sat down in the chair and read the witness statement that whatever they were about to ask me to do would probably not end well for me.

I'm not trying to give away the story, or add a touch of fatalism to the investigation I am about to recount; instead I'm trying to give you a sense of what it feels like and what it really means to be an investigator.

That is, the implications of looking into the soul of a city that I knew from experience had an uncanny ability to compromise the law in the pursuit of vice.

I had worked plainclothes and developed a pretty good sense of how money from illicit businesses like prostitution and gambling found its way into the coffers of seemingly legitimate enterprises. So I knew at that moment, that delving into this crime would put me on an island of sorts, a friendless way station where you have few friends and plenty of enemies.

Let me explain why.

There was an alleged numbers man who our witness knew was making payoffs to a then unnamed high level Baltimore City police officer, a man who the witness said had the power to make things "go away."

And that's when the sixth sense kicked in. I mean, it's pretty obvious that investigating a police officer is not a choice job. It's almost a cliché to say that working the 1966 version of internal affairs was not a way to win friends and get promoted. However it wasn't cops going after cops that made me wary.

What my sixth sense told me, was that if a high ranking officer was involved, then quite likely a whole bunch of other people with influence, connections and ways to make an investigator's life miserable could also be on the take. And that was why I knew I was in for it.

Still, even though I had my doubts, what could I really say? Judge Moylan was a mentor, one of the best legal minds in the city who taught me both respect for and how to use the law effectively. Plus the case was the type of challenge that a good investigator lives for.

And maybe, to be honest, it was the type of case I lived for. Who knows what drives a person to do things that you know may end badly? It's sort of like career vertigo, you want to jump in feet first even though there is nothing but hardening concrete that awaits you.

So I said Yes. And as it turns out, I was an idiot.

INTERNAL AFFAIRS

Remember that in 1966 the Internal Affairs Division was a new idea, so cops weren't used to being watched. In fact, there was little if any independent oversight of the department.

And then of course, you have the simple fact that everyone loves to gamble, and a whole lot of powerful people love the profit it generates.

At that time the city was awash in the numbers racket — illegal lotteries that worked just like the current legal version, just a little less conspicuous. In fact, it wasn't until 1973 that the state created its own lottery, a move that was the beginning of the end for the illegal numbers business.

But at that time, if you wanted to buy a lottery ticket, the numbers racket was your game. You can imagine given the hundreds of millions of dollars the state rakes in currently year in and year out, that even then it was a big business.

A business I was about to wade into in search of a crooked high-ranking cop, no less.

But back to the case.

As I said from the outset, the cast of characters I met at the Criminal Justice Commission was hardly your typical investigation team.

For one thing, the *Sun* reporter had taken the unusual step of bringing the witness to us in the first place. And now he wanted to be involved in the investigation — not necessarily standard procedure, to say the least.

Let's face it, the goal of a cop and the job of a reporter are often at odds. I have a lot of respect for the First Amendment, but a criminal investigation is something to write about after the fact, not during.

However since the reporter effectively brought the case to us, he wanted in, and he got his wish. The next sticky question was operational. How would I conduct an investigation of high-level cops without someone getting wind of it?

We hatched a plan whereby I would be quietly detailed to a

private detective agency in Roland Park. The idea was for me to simply fade away: I couldn't tell anyone what I was working on, not even my supervisors.

Basically, I was on my own. And whatever happened in the course of this investigation, the blowback would be on me.

Welcome to the world of the investigator.

And so, with little fanfare, one witness and a reporter in tow, I began to work on a case that would not only shake the department to its core, but even prompt significant changes to the way we did business.

SURVEILLANCE

So a few weeks later I found myself in the offices of the International Detective Agency, an outfit run by a former army intelligence officer named Marshall Myers.

Detailed to me were two city cops, one who I will call "Sam," a cop who would become a major thorn in my side later on.

The evidence outlined in the witness statements was a start, but not nearly enough.

The first witness had provided a sketchy link between cops and gambling on Pennsylvania Avenue: She had worked for numbers man Phil Taylor. And while she was not directly involved in the operation, she was close friends with Taylor and thus had overheard details of his wheeling and dealing, details that piqued my interest.

While she didn't want to specifically talk about cops being involved in illegal lotteries, she did know that Taylor was making payoffs to several officers, including one who lived in Baltimore County and drove a nice car, and whose house had a swimming pool.

The payoffs were big, she said. One month's worth of bribes would be enough for her to live comfortably on for a year.

In fact, this witness told the commission she was sure police were involved in the illegal lottery business, but that there was little point in reporting crooked cops because too many were involved.

However she was not the only witness who had firsthand knowledge of police involvement in lotteries, specifically the Pennsylvania Avenue operation.

After talking to several other witnesses, the same two names kept coming up, a lieutenant and a sergeant in the Detective Division.

And there was one witness in particular who had quite a story. Her name was Ida May Pryor, a middle aged woman from East Baltimore.

According to the statement she gave us, one night the lieutenant and sergeant showed up at her house with a box. Her daughter answered the door, and called Ida May downstairs because she mistakenly thought the cops had brought them some food.

But it turned out the duo had nothing of the sort. Instead, they stormed into the house and started rummaging through the Pryors' freezer. Ida May asked the sergeant — whose name was Riggs — if he was in some kind of trouble.

"No," Riggs said. "I just need you to hold something for me," he explained.

It turns out that "something" was roughly $12,000 cash and a box of numbers slips, the take from a day of illegal numbers-running down on Pennsylvania Avenue.

He didn't offer any explanation as to why he needed to stash the lottery receipts in her refrigerator, after which he simply disappeared.

The two men also asked if her daughter had bought a number, No. 541.

"Yes," she told them.

Had it been paid off, one of the detectives asked?

"No," she said.

And then things got really odd.

Not only did the duo talk to her about the cash, but they said they thought Willy Diggs and an associate named Salisbury should pay off on the number, a total of 12 grand. They said it was the only way to maintain their reputation in the numbers business. One of the cops even threatened to hurt Diggs if he got his hands on him.

It was enough to suggest the officers weren't investigating Diggs, but were working in the same business.

And who were these two police officers with what appeared to be a stake in the numbers racket?

It was the very same lieutenant and sergeant that had been mentioned as being on the take by several other witnesses: two high ranking officers from the Detective Division who appeared to be knee deep in the numbers racket.

The investigation into the Western District supervisors progressed, so we began regular surveillance of the 1500 block of Pennsylvania Avenue.

Unlike tracking down drug dealers or other types of low level criminals, when you go after cops you have to be cautious. First of all, cops know all the tricks of the trade, so trying to infiltrate a criminal enterprise run by police is pretty risky business.

That's why we decided consistent surveillance of the location was our best option.

Using two vans equipped with 8-millimeter movie cameras, we parked with a good view of the entire block. We watched and we filmed.

Let's just say it didn't take long for us to get a real sense of what was going on.

From morning until evening every day a lawyer's office and a bar called the York Hotel were awash with people — not just ordinary citizens but cops as well.

In and out all day, the officers and a veritable Who's Who of the city's underground gambling racket were seen entering and leaving the buildings where the lotteries were run.

We couldn't see exactly what was going on inside, but even from our vantage point on the street we could see paper slips being exchanged hand to hand — lots of them.

In my first intelligence report to then-Captain Vincent Gavin, we counted roughly 167 people entering the York Hotel and Snack Bar in less than two hours. I reported that the traffic was so heavy on the block that it was hard to get descriptions.

One of those 167 people was a man known as Mickey Mixup, a well-known lottery lieutenant for Julius Salisbury, the man who was technically responsible for the paying of the No. 541 ticket belonging to the daughter of our witness.

We also noticed there was an ebb and flow to the traffic: heavy in the morning until noon, and then resuming heavy from two in the afternoon until five o'clock. In between, the foot traffic could be counted on a single hand.

So in my report, I made it clear we believed that these locations were being used for an illegal lottery operation, a conclusion I immortalized in a memo to Captain Gavin several weeks into the investigation.

Meanwhile, the *Sun* reporter was asking for a wire so he could follow what he described as a hot lead. According to him, a gang member working out of Baltimore's red light district known as The Block was helping the cops stash some of the gambling proceeds.

But despite giving the reporter full support and backup, his so-called leads typically turned up nothing but dead ends. The key witness or the groundbreaking statement was always just around the corner, he would say. Not a single statement or witness he promised to deliver ever materialized during the investigation.

So I started to believe the reporter was playing us, or else he was trying to keep us interested in what he had to say in order to maintain the inside scoop on where the investigation was headed.

I discussed my suspicions with Commissioner Gelston and told him in no uncertain terms that I thought the reporter was a threat to the investigation. In short, I wanted to put a tail on him.

Gelston agreed.

So I assigned two of my men to follow him — and it didn't take long to get results.

Just one day later my two cops watched as he engaged in a fairly intricate sex act with one of our original witnesses.

Sitting in a car under JFX Rte. 83 not far from the offices of the *Baltimore Sun*, the blissfully unaware reporter seemed to be having an extremely intimate relationship with the woman whom he brought to the Justice Commission just a month before.

And not only did we catch them in the car, but later we observed him entering her home early the next evening and then leaving the following morning.

I reported the dalliance to Commissioner Gelston, who quickly arranged a meeting with the reporter's editor at *The Sun*. Needless to say the reporter soon vanished. I don't know if he was fired, transferred or what, but the man never showed up asking questions again.

His foibles however were just a minor distraction to our case. Surveillance was paying off. We had pretty much established the fact that Pennsylvania Avenue was the central headquarters of a large illegal numbers operation. Even better, with the testimony from Ida May we were on the way to linking the operation to the lieutenant and sergeant from the Detective Bureau.

In fact, we had caught a number of cops from the Western District leaving and entering businesses on Pennsylvania Avenue which served as the apparent logistical headquarters for the illegal lottery.

So with the evidence from surveillance coupled with several strong witness statements, we asked for and received the approval of State's Attorney Moylan to construct a warrant.

Now if you recall, at the beginning of this chapter I mentioned that I knew going in that this case was bound to be trouble. I had an investigator's premonition that things were going to fall apart.

It was not long after I wrote the warrants to search the businesses along that active stretch of Pennsylvania Avenue, that they did.

THE DISAPPEARING WARRANT

It all started with the catchphrase that was my unofficial career mantra. I would employ it with mindless repetition to get it through the thick skulls of cops: how important it is to learn, know, and follow the law. Something I repeated so many times at the city's Police Training Academy, cadets accused me of having dementia.

Get a warrant, get a warrant, get a warrant.

With more than enough evidence that the 1500 block of Pennsylvania Avenue was a mecca for illegal numbers, I began to write the warrants for searches on several businesses where we had observed excessive foot traffic, the mercurial characters slipping in and out like ghosts, and the constant shuffling of slips of paper from hand to hand.

As discussed earlier in this book, at that time there was no formal training for Baltimore City police officers with regard to writing warrants. In fact, 1966 was the first year that we had what is known as in-service training — time taken off the beat to brush up on things like the law, though the law was hardly the central focus.

Most of what I learned about writing warrants I learned from judges like Charles Moylan. And now I had to write one hell of a warrant, because I was about to walk into what I assumed from my investigation were some pretty well-connected businesses.

This dilemma, having to learn one of the most basic skills of criminal investigations on the fly, is one of the reasons I'm writing this book. There is a more detailed chapter on the law earier in the book but there is no better teacher than a real-life example. This case is definitive of how important a well-written warrant can be.

Any good defense attorney will go over the warrant with a fine tooth comb, looking to find factual errors, for example. Or in some cases, nullify an arrest simply because you didn't have a warrant in the first place.

If he or she is successful, then all the evidence you discovered and confiscated, and all the ensuing leads you developed from the search can technically be tossed out the window. If your warrant or your search is no good, you are going to have trouble.

Of course, that's not what happened in this case. It was in fact worse.

As I stated before, I wrote warrants for several businesses on the block where we had observed and filmed the heavy foot-traffic and the slips of paper exchanging hands.

Just before the raid I received an unusual order from Captain Gavin: he wanted me to use the Western District Plainclothes Squad to conduct it.

I was a little taken aback.

First of all, the Western District Plainclothes Squad was run by a lieutenant who I didn't think would take kindly to being ordered around by a sergeant. Second, some of the men in the squad were caught on our surveillance footage of the block. In other words, some of the same cops who might be the target of our investigation would be taking part in a raid to uncover evidence of their misdeeds.

Remember when I said at the beginning of this chapter that this case would be trouble?

Of course, I didn't have a choice. Following orders is not optional in the Baltimore Police Department, even when the orders are misguided.

So there I was, standing in the parking lot of the old Memorial Stadium with a truck, a set of freshly written warrants, and the entire Plainclothes Squad of the Western District standing around scratching their heads.

Since I already knew some of the officers in the squad could be at least tacitly involved in these gambling operations, I knew it was possible they would be tempted to tip off the numbers businesses we were about to raid. So I didn't tell them anything about where we were headed before they were all sitting in the truck and the doors were locked.

Fortunately there were no cellphones in those days.

Now I can't exactly describe how the men looked when I passed around the warrants. Let's just say the term "pale as a ghost" doesn't do it justice. I mean, at that moment they held in their hands warrants to raid several illicit numbers businesses which some of the same men in the truck had been visiting regularly.

Contributing to their evident dismay was the fact that the warrants described how we knew the targeted establishments were home to illegal lotteries — the surveillance film.

So needless to say it was not a happy crew assembled in the truck headed toward one of the biggest search and seizure raids of my career.

But little did I know how the unhappy few would strike back.

When we arrived on Pennsylvania Avenue the officers disembarked from the truck and spread out over the block like a flock of angry seagulls. Then, as the cops entered the businesses to execute the warrants, people from all the shops began to file out onto the street, bewildered.

It wasn't an unruly mob, just a large crowd of customers, office workers, and of course the dumbfounded numbers men. They seemed unable to reconcile the fact that the same police department which had been up until now buttressing their illegal gambling operation was suddenly rummaging through their files and gathering evidence to put them in jail.

I can't say that I witnessed any direct confrontations between my men and the suspects, but I'm sure there were plenty of awkward moments when a cop on the take ran headfirst into one of the people who were paying him off.

Fortunately the raid was successful and we gathered lots of evidence. We pulled boxes of the number slips and receipts. We found cash and records indicating that the 1500 block of Pennsylvania Avenue was indeed a numbers racket mecca.

Things were looking up, at least for a couple of hours.

But shortly after the raid was concluded, and I started to collect the original warrants, that's when things began to fall apart.

When a police officer conducts a raid of a home, business, or any other space where the Constitution requires we obtain legal permission to enter, the officer leaves a copy of the warrant at the location and brings the original back to the police district where the raid occurred. The warrant is then filed away in a drawer to be presented in court at trial, a practice which actually changed later on because of what happened next.

So after the raid was concluded I did what I always do, gather the original copies of the warrant for the court file. The only problem was, one of the officers, "Sam," said he didn't know where the basic warrant was.

"What do you mean you don't have the warrant?" I remember saying to Sam a bit heatedly standing on Pennsylvania Avenue. But he just shrugged his shoulders and stared up at the sky.

Let me be clear here that warrants aren't something a cop misplaces like a set of car keys or a wallet. When you're conducting a raid it's the most important item in your possession, even more so than your gun. An entire case, including all the evidence collected, can hinge on conducting a proper search.

And any proper search begins and ends with a warrant.

So when Sam stood on Pennsylvania Avenue claiming he lost the warrant, I was not only dumbfounded, I was beyond angry. I knew he was trying to set me up. Not only that, he was showing complete disregard for the law.

Realizing then that this could screw up the entire case, I immediately called State's Attorney Moylan. He too was outraged. So outraged, in fact, he called the police commissioner and asked that Sam be fired.

But that was just the beginning of the treachery.

Unknown to me at the time, one of the men from the Western District Plainclothes Squad who assisted me in conducting the raid was caught counseling suspects on prospective lawyers.

It was unreal.

So here I had one cop hiding a warrant and another trying to give suspects tips on how to beat the rap.

But at least the raid produced evidence — solid evidence.

In one barbershop we confiscated slips containing 19 bets at $4.25 a pop. In another we found 112 numbers for bets totaling $79 and another box of slips with 160 bets and $131. In a bar entered by Sam and another plainclothes officer, more betting slips and cash were discovered.

But the cop who accompanied Sam also said he thought he saw a plainclothes officer sitting next to one of the suspects, an officer who apparently slipped out the back door before anyone bothered to question him or let me know about it.

The alleged cop slipped out before the warrant was served to suspect James Jackson Jr., who was coincidentally holding roughly $2,600 cash and corresponding betting slips.

Five suspects in all, including Jackson, were charged. But it was the disappearance of the warrant and the cast of characters who made an appearance on our 8-millimeter films that turned this case into a high and holy mess.

While we were preparing for trial, the word got out that it was none other than the original two, the sergeant and lieutenant whose "repo" job was to get back $12,000 in cash, captured on our surveillance footage.

And they weren't the only ones.

Three other Western District officers starred in the film, along with two corrections officers and a probation agent. It was, to say the least, a broad spectrum of representatives from law enforcement.

The raid netted enough evidence to charge five men with running an illegal gambling operation, but the police officers were another story.

Shortly after the raid the lieutenant retired, and just before I was about to interview the sergeant, I was ordered by newly named Commissioner Donald Pomerleau to drop it.

It was not an enviable position to be in. I'd just caught a bunch of cops more than likely committing crimes. I was now the face of an investigation that had revealed an ugly truth about the City of Baltimore: the cozy relationship between cops and the city's illicit gambling business.

And now, as I predicted, I was being prevented from finishing the job.

But it would get worse.

The trial for the five men was a big media event. Not only because we'd busted a pretty large numbers operation in the heart of the city or because five well-known numbers runners were facing serious criminal charges.

What made the trial big news was who wasn't on trial, which was the elephant in the room that drew everyone's curiosity. It was the cops caught on film and the rumors that police were involved but never fully investigated, which made the trial more than a local curiosity.

Remember, I stated earlier in this chapter that I could smell trouble when this case was first presented to me. And it was one of my own men who threw the first proverbial punch, absconding with the original warrant. But nothing prepared me for what happened next.

The day I was scheduled to testify I had brought a copy, not the original, of the warrant with me. It was the best I could do because the original had never been found.

The prosecution team knew that the defense would make an issue of the fact that the original warrant was missing. I was simply hoping that a copy would be enough.

But believe it or not, before I could finish my testimony about our surveillance and the raid, the copy of the warrant — which had been sitting in the jury room — went missing.

It's hard to believe that a warrant on an explosive case like this would be stolen not once, but twice. And who would commit such a brazen act? All I know to this day is that there were six cops in that jury room, six suspects. Even today I don't know which officer stole it.

But then things got really strange.

Outside the courthouse, a reporter from *The Sun* approached me.

"I know what happened to your warrant," he told me.

"Well then, tell me," was all I could say, not believing that once again a *Sun* reporter was knee deep in my case.

"Ask my editor," he replied.

So during the lunch break I made my way over to the *Sun* headquarters on Calvert Street, a few blocks north of the courthouse.

The meeting didn't last long. "I'm not going to tell you how I got it, but I have your warrant," the editor told me.

I couldn't believe it, there in his hand, was the original warrant I had given to Sam just before the raid. The missing warrant which had thrown a monkey wrench into the biggest case of my life had somehow ended up in the offices of a newspaper.

We didn't exchange but a few words, I was due back in court.

Once I arrived I quickly found Charles Moylan told him what happened. He was, to say the least, dumbfounded.

"Where the hell did you get that?" he asked, completely baffled by the sudden turn of events.

"From an editor at *The Sun*," I told him.

I do have some idea how the warrant got into the hands of the media, but it's hearsay and I can't prove it, so I don't want to detail it here.

The truth is, the fact that the warrant ended up in the hands of a reporter rather than a cop tells you something about this case, and the city itself.

Obviously there were police involved in the illegal gambling, in other words committing crimes serious enough to warrant an in-depth investigation. But in the end, the corrupt forces inside the department won out.

And to a certain extent even though we recovered the warrant and presented it in court, the damage had already been done.

Initially we thought we would have to prosecute the case without the original warrant, and so the prosecutors decided to show the film of Pennsylvania Avenue during the presentation of their case. It was a tough call because that evidence tipped our hand and let everyone know what we knew.

Although I was sequestered while the film was shown in court, I was told you could see the shadows of people leaving the court-room as their images were projected onto the screen.

Yes, we had solid proof that corruption was a serious problem inside the police department.

Yes, we had evidence of ongoing illegal activities of a number of law enforcement personnel. But that's not what the court ulti-mately focused on.

In the end, after the five men were convicted, Judge Joseph L. Carter asked Commissioner Pomerleau to conduct an internal investigation into the disappearance of the warrant.

Pomerleau then told the press he would look into — and I'm quoting directly here — "all aspects or integrity, or lack of integ-rity, on the part of police officers."

And guess who he focused on? Me, of course.

As I said at the beginning, I knew in the end that this investiga-tion could turn back on me in a heartbeat.

Given that cops and influential people were involved, and that money and gambling were fueling it, there was no doubt I was in trouble.

It really wasn't a surprise to me then. When you seek out the truth in a community where the truth is unwelcome, there's bound to be a reaction. Many times during my career I was criticized for not knowing when to stop. And this was one of the investigations where it seems I didn't.

The fallout was, of course, swift.

A major who didn't like me was put in charge. After I filed my report on the missing warrant he created a list of a hundred questions about the investigation and the missing warrant that I had ordered.

Truthfully it seemed like a trap; the wording and the language were too precise.

So I secretly obtained counsel, answered each question in sequence, and carefully.

It infuriated the major, who accused me of consulting a lawyer. Which of course I did.

On the surface I was investigated for failure to manage my troops, for losing the warrant, and also for not keeping a closer eye on Sam.

But in the end, I was simply a scapegoat for the ugliness that a jury and a room full of top brass couldn't handle.

Someone had to take the fall for the ugly picture of policing presented in that courtroom, and it was me.

Eventually I was cleared of any wrongdoing. But that didn't stop Pomerleau from calling me every name in the book as I sat in his office just a few weeks later. It was an hour-long tirade during which he questioned my character, integrity and ability, using expletives as adjectives.

"You will never work in plainclothes again," he promised. His concession was to allow me to choose the district where I would be working as a sergeant in uniform.

His tongue-lashing was one of the most humiliating experiences of my life. Afterwards I remember one of my mentors, Captain George Duechler, who was present during Pomerleau's tirade, asking me how I could just sit there and take the abuse.

I simply told him I had four children and a wife to take care of. At the time I had only a seventh grade education, and policing was something I was good at.

But that doesn't mean I wasn't angry. Or that adversity doesn't sometimes reap rewards.

Maybe that was the moment I decided to go back to school, a decision that would not only lead to obtaining the high school diploma that I lacked, but a college degree, a master's, and several advanced certificates from Loyola University.

Maybe it just taught me a lesson that when you delve into the corrupt sinew of a community, that you're on your own. An investigator, in the end, is really an island unto himself. That when you pull back the curtain on the corrupt elements in society, the person who holds it is often made the scapegoat.

It's like being an unpopular prophet: if people don't like the message, they find ways to discredit the messenger.

But there was something else beneficial about my first wide-ranging investigation of cops.

There was a lesson from the investigation that stuck with me through 60-odd years of law enforcement. A lesson that would get me through the hard times and difficulties of going where no one wants you to go and where no one is willing to face the truth.

It was a lesson that to this day I would share with anyone who walks the path of an investigator.

Wait. Be patient.

Because the tables will turn, as they surely did for me.

CHAPTER NINE: KILLING ISN'T EASY

The Day I Shot a Man Who Died

Are you capable of killing?

Let me rephrase that: If push came to shove, could you kill someone? Even if you're staring down the barrel of a gun, could you snuff out a life? Could you make the decision to wipe someone off the face of the earth in a matter of seconds?

Take a minute and think; it's not as easy as it sounds.

I mean, it looks easy for movie stars like Bruce Willis or Arnold Schwarzenegger as they mow down 30 people in 10 minutes of jump-cut adrenaline at your local duplex. It's pretty painless when you're a virtual couch soldier playing call-of-duty picking off pixilated Nazis with the push of a button.

But it's a whole different story when the victim is flesh and blood. Watching a living, breathing human turn into a stiffened bloody corpse the second after you pull the trigger ain't the same as seeing a bad guy get shot in the head on your widescreen television or in the movie theater.

It's just not as easy to take a life when you can't give it back.

I raise this question because while I've witnessed a great deal of violence in my career, none of it resembles the grist for the televisual mill that populates current popular culture. The dying and killing we consume is as substantive as cotton candy. It's a confection: championship wrestling with a dash of sugar.

And that troubles me.

Because that gap in firsthand experience in part drives our boundless thirst for it. I think we embrace violence in this country as a solution for so many problems because we have so little firsthand experience with it.

It's why police adapt military-style tactics in poor, dysfunctional neighborhoods. It drives the call for more cops, more prisons, and more enforcement every time crime spikes. It's the reason SWAT teams evolve into tactical units and tactical units stockpile assault weapons like an army division. It drives our hunger for retribution, turning justice into a collective act of reprisal.

But as someone who has wiped a human being off the face of this earth forever, I can say that violence is complicated. And killing is fraught with unintended consequences. It's not something you ever learn to live with; it lives with you.

I mean it's easy to pull a trigger. It's easy to fire off a few rounds in the heat of the moment when you're staring down the barrel of a gun. It's even easy to justify after the fact. Particularly if the person you killed has a violent criminal history.

But to live with it, to kill and then go about your life, is a different proposition altogether. And it's something worth thinking about if we're going to ask people with guns to solve our problems.

I know, because I've killed.

NAKED PURSUIT

March 22, 1962.

The day I was promoted to sergeant.

It was, to say the least, unexpected; a pleasant surprise for a beat cop used to being upbraided, not rewarded.

In fact, I was 257th on the list of potential candidates, pretty much near the bottom.

So when commissioner Bernard Schmidt suddenly appeared at Western District Headquarters to inform me I had made the cut, it was one of those rare moments in policing when things actually work out better than you expect. It was a welcome step up for a man who had four mouths at home to feed.

Nevertheless, I didn't have time to savor the moment; I was due out on patrol.

I'd been working plainclothes focusing on commercial robberies with my then-partner, Officer Mark Elliot. There'd been a rash of stickups along Mosher Street, so we were cruising the area with hopes of catching someone in the act. Basic police work: put people where crime occurs — to observe, then apprehend.

That's when I saw what at first glance looked so absurd I thought I was hallucinating.

On the corner of North Carrollton Avenue and Mosher, a man emerged from a side door of a corner grocery store dressed only in his underwear. The reluctant streaker had pushed open a side door before spilling onto the sidewalk and scrambling down the street, hands tied behind his back.

While Elliot rushed to help the unclothed victim, I hightailed it toward an alley off Carrollton. Call it a hunch, but it looked like a robbery. I'd learned working this beat that the legion of armed robbers who hit Mosher Street tended to head south, then circle back around to survey the aftermath.

So I ran down the street as fast as I could, my heart beating a million times a second. It was the type of moment that embodies the best and worst of policing. Boredom transformed by a foot chase into a minute of terrifying excitement.

Now when I say excitement , I mean that if you don't get a bit juiced by chasing down a guy who just robbed someone, you shouldn't be a cop. It's the nature of the beast. You have to be motivated by the hunt, the impulse to put a man away who has done someone wrong.

On the other hand, once you've been on the streets, you learn that things can go bad in an instant, and I mean really bad. Deadly bad.

So, full of adrenaline, I turned into the alley.

That's when I spotted him, the man who would change my life forever. He was holding a bag in one hand — and a gun in the other.

He was about 20 feet away from me trying to force his way through the back door of a row home. Just a man and a bag. A suspect and a threat. A criminal committing a crime. A man holding a gun.

So I pulled my gun while he spun around. We locked eyes. It was a brief moment of mutual recognition. That split second of lucidity that only seems real after the fact.

He wanted to get away; I was set on cuffing him. He was on the verge of escape; I was the foil. It was like a sizing up of all the possibilities in the blink of an eye: freedom or arrest, failure or success; and lastly death.

He chose the latter.

He raised the gun and pointed it, a slight flick of the wrist that caught my eye. It was just enough of a threat to prompt me to pull the trigger.

I fired just one shot, in the blinking of an eye. I was a split second faster — fast enough not to die.

In that instant, his fierce, defiant expression melted into a look of blank surprise — like he couldn't believe I did it. I could see blood spurting from his groin. He let out an excruciating yelp like a wounded dog, and then pushed his way into the row home.

I pursued.

Inside, a family was eating dinner, abruptly glancing up from their plates of meatloaf and potatoes to see a bleeding man in the early throes of death stumbling through their kitchen, wailing in pain.

This is where my partner caught up with him. Or to be more precise, watched as he burst out of the house, tumbled onto the front sidewalk and collapsed, though not yet dead.

And that was it.

In literally less than a minute, little more than the blinking of an eye in the overall scheme of things, less than the time of your average television commercial, I had been transformed from an average beat cop into a potential killer. Not a killer without cause, mind you, or justification. But still a man who had in the blink of an eye most likely just taken the life of another.

They rushed the perpetrator to the hospital, but I had a feeling he was going to die. He'd left a trail of blood so thick you could smell it.

I'd like to say I didn't care because I knew the shot was justified. Or that it didn't bother me a bit that a man who had just pointed a gun at me was lying on his deathbed gurney.

But that's not true. Yes, I felt lucky to be alive. The man had a gun and was going to use it. Against me. But I was trained to shoot first. I was trained to survive.

Still, I had doubts. The kind of doubts that start racing through your mind almost as quickly as the adrenaline recedes.

Had I been too quick to pull the trigger? Did I make the right decision? Could this have played out differently, in a less final, fatal way? And even more troubling, who was this man, this person I encountered in a back alley? This criminal who forced me to make the most consequential decision of my life without even thinking?

My heart still pounding, I tried to calm myself by replaying the shooting over and over in my mind. I'd seen the gun, I'd watched his hand twitch. I'd noticed all the predispositions of a man on the precipice of violence.

And I responded as I was trained. All too effectively, it seemed. What else could I have done? What else *should* I have done?

If you shoot someone, and you're not a sociopath, this is where it starts. These are the questions that start to replay in your mind. It's the voice of doubt which repeats like a broken record, an ongoing dialogue with yourself, parsing options that no longer exist. A subconscious squabble that leads to a quick rendezvous with cop schizophrenia.

And therein lies the rub of shooting a man, the difference between wasting flesh and blood and plying a virtual corpse. When you watch a man diced with your own bullet turn white as a sheet of virgin snow it's not so easy to stomach.

Only a nutcase wouldn't feel conflicted.

THE HOLE-IN-ONE CLUB

Thankfully, I didn't have too much time to wrestle with it; paperwork was waiting.

When I got back to District Headquarters, I picked up a pen and started filling out reports — lots of them. One minute of action recounted in three days' worth of writing. It was a painstaking rehash of every detail. The dull end of the blade, so the speak, justifying everything on paper.

I was sitting at a desk just getting started when Captain Wade Poole suddenly appeared.

"Welcome to the hole-in-one club," he said with a wry smile. "That son of a bitch just died."

And that was that, the final verdict: I was a killer. Even though I expected it, I was still stunned. I didn't know the guy, I had no idea if the world was better off with him or without him. All I knew for sure was that he spent the last three minutes of his life bleeding out from a wound inflicted by me.

And I couldn't help wondering about him, the man I shot. Who was he? A stone cold killer or a junky with a habit? A violent sociopath or just a two-bit holdup man? In other words, did he deserve it?

Even if he was Hitler in the making, did I have a right to end his life?

Sure, he decided to point a gun at me. Sure, he made the decision to rob a convenience store. Yes, it was his bad decision-making that contrived our fatal rendezvous. But was it behavior worthy of a death sentence?

Bottom line, I had killed a man, and there was nothing I could do to make it feel easier.

It's the finality of it that gets you. You make a bad arrest, and the suspect can win his freedom from a jury. You focus on the wrong suspect, and an experienced prosecutor can point you in the right direction. Cops make mistakes, many of which can be fixed.

But not taking a life. It's the irrevocable part that rushes over you like a tide of misapprehension. The more you think, the more you replay the shot in your mind, the more doubt can creep in.

CHARGED LIKE A CRIMINAL

Making matters worse, shootings were treated quite differently in the 1960s. We didn't have any of the protection afforded officers today.

First, I was suspended without pay. No administrative leave or paid desk duty, no taking it easy while I waited for judgment. Put simply, I was ordered to hand over my gun and badge, no questions asked.

One minute, you're facing death; the next, you're not even a cop, I thought to myself as I handed over my service revolver to the captain.

There was no paycheck for the four hungry mouths at home and a wife without an income. Not a single dime while I waited in a less than hospitable occupational purgatory for cops who shoot people.

But living without a paycheck was just one problem. Back then, if you shot someone in the line of duty, you were automatically charged with a crime. Seriously, there was a presumption of guilt. Imagine putting on a uniform one day, and then standing in front of a judge a few hours later who says matter of factly, "You are charged with homicide by shooting."

That's exactly what happened to me.

In fact, the captain had to go in front of the judge with a writ of habeas corpus to keep me out of jail.

And so my fate was in the hands of the court. I could be a murderer, or a police officer. I could be a killer, or a hero. Today officers keep their pay, and their badge. But me, the primary breadwinner with the aforementioned four hungry children was shit-out-of-luck.

It's a bitch of a life. A split-second decision to pull the trigger, analyzed and scrutinized by people who have all the time in the world. Hesitate and you get shot yourself. Pull the trigger to save your own life, and you end up in front of a judge. Either way you're screwed.

And I was.

To make matters even worse, my promotion was put on hold.

So there I was, a killer, a suspended cop, without a paycheck, awaiting uncertain judgment. It was quite a predicament for a man barely 30 years of age.

And of course, along with all the legal headaches were the aforementioned ruminations of doubt. A sense of unease that made every other part of the process appear trivial by comparison. I wanted to know I did the right thing. It just had to make sense.

Welcome to the real consequences of killing.

A PERILOUS PAPER TRAIL

Anyway, I had to do something. I couldn't just sit on my hands and stew. So I turned to the skill set that had bailed me out more than once in my fledgling career: the instinct for figuring things out that always kept me on the beat. My core competency, so to speak.

Investigating.

In this case, investigating the past of the man I shot. It was the best salve for my conscience that I could muster.

So I pulled the files and located the police reports. I did the legwork — without the aid of computers — and assembled a healthy paper trail. I rummaged through the files in the basement of Western District Headquarters, fighting with rats and spiders for significant scraps of paper.

And what I managed to wrestle from the dustbins was a picture of a man with a habit of picking up a gun and pointing it at people. A habit so ingrained he'd done it on record more than once. Several times in fact.

I discovered he'd been implicated in a series of armed robberies around West Baltimore, three of which ended with the man I shot shooting someone else. In other words he was a killer in the making. He was a sociopath who had shot to kill more than once — a powder keg with a gun, hell-bent on self-destruction.

In truth, he was a menace, a deadly threat.

So for better or worse it was possible, maybe even likely, I had saved someone else's life, the split second decision to shoot a man in a back alley, a win of sorts. I couldn't ask for a better back story. It was the most definitive outcome I could have hoped for. A violent man with a violent past felled before he could hurt someone else.

At least that's the tale I told myself that helped me get over it, in part.

As for the judge, he agreed; my verdict: not guilty. And the shooting was "justified." My badge and gun, returned.

Riding the bus to the Western District the day after my trial, I saw my name in the paper. I was indeed promoted to sergeant.

Still, it was a harrowing process. Putting cops on trial for pulling the trigger should only happen in the most extreme circumstances. Doubts can be fatal, particularly when guns are involved. That's the thing about putting people with deadly weapons on the streets to solve problems. Sometimes people die.

Real people.

Of course this is all small talk. The fact remains that killing a man, even if he's led a life of crime, isn't easy to deal with. You can act like it's just part of the job, but it isn't. It's like pretending the tales of violence that inhabit our television sets depict killing as it really is, a plentiful feast of blood with no aftertaste.

It's a fallacy and a lie. Because killing a person is the most profound act imaginable. It's never easy, or at least it shouldn't be.

It certainly wasn't for me.

CHAPTER TEN:
THE BOOK OF COP

*The Plot to Kill a Commissioner
That Started with a Joke*

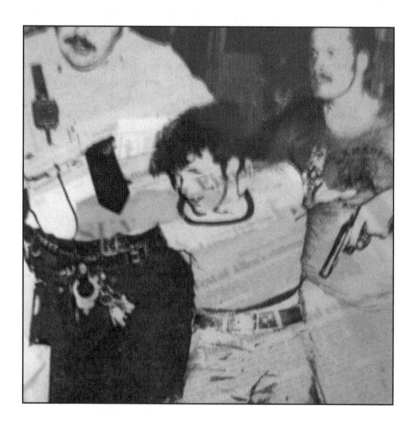

YOU CAN'T STOP MURDER

I've tried in this book to convey what it means to be a cop, for better or worse.

How it feels to aim a gun at another human being, and pull the trigger. Why it hurts to take a life. What it means to cuff a rapist. The sense of betrayal you feel when you're immersed in an investigation, only to find yourself at the wrong end of it, and your job on the line.

The idea is to offer an insider's perspective. The truth as I experienced it. A dose of reality about the inherent contradictions of enforcing laws, written and broken by human beings.

But getting inside the world of policing is just part of the reason I'm writing this book. Admittedly, a bunch of old war stories told by an aging cop is hardly worth the trouble, if the occupation that defines it goes unexamined.

So I've also looked in the mirror, I've turned the spotlight on myself. I've tried to question my own beliefs, and most of all re-examine the whole idea of what it means to be a cop. For want of a better term, I would call this the Book of Cop: The ugly liturgy of policing, a compilation of meager truths and bitter pills, some swallowed, some not.

The Book of Cop.

In it, you'll find the essence of the job, in all its particularities and contradictions. The joy of an occupation rooted in the extremes of human behavior, and the administrative orthodoxies which consume it.

And as such, no Book of Cop would be complete without acknowledging the great leveling force which undermines us at every turn.

Absurdity.

That's right, the absurd. It's a word which terrorizes cops. The insolent curse that turns rules, procedures, laws and good intentions into a mix of chaos and futility.

It is, in essence, how things really happen, not how we think, hope or plan they will happen. It's the bane of the mundane arrest turned violent, the futile car stop where everything that can possibly go wrong, does. It's the unseen force that scrambles the cop universe into a stew of entropy.

The absurd.

You think I'm kidding? Over-dramatizing?

What if I told you I was asked to investigate a threat involving a high-profile city official, an office boss, based solely upon a joke?

That's right, a full-throttle, full-scale murder-for-hire probe prompted by a couple of minutes of offhand sarcasm. And what if the supervisor who ordered me to handle it had recently said I would never again work as a detective so long as he was my boss? He had closed the door on my career as a detective for good.

That is, until someone told a joke. A joke, a really bad joke.

Well it's true, and as you'll see, it's a case which proves my point of how the process of enforcing the law can often upend order and undermine good intentions.

But before I muse more upon the absurd, let me relay the bungled attempt at humor that started the chain of stupidity that ended up on my lap.

It emerged from a conversation that took place at the old Lord Baltimore Hotel in Room 938 on July 15th, 1974, the content of which was passed along to me in the form of an interoffice memo. I'll simply transcribe the snippets of conversation as it was presented to me so you can judge for yourself.

Speaker one: "Well I better go look for a job, this one is shot."

Speaker two: "Yeah man, well, I look at it this way — six years ago I was looking for work; I guess I can do it now, but what a fucking shame."

Speaker three: "I'm not going to worry about it because I'll jump right out this window. I hope I land on one of those 'scab' cars so they have to write a report."

Speaker four: "I'm collecting $10 donations for a 'contract' and we'll get him killed."

Speaker five: "Well I guess this is it. I wonder what I'll be doing two weeks from now."

Speaker six: "If I'm fired, I don't have to worry where I'll be because I already know where I'll be."

Several minutes later more people entered Room 938 and joined the conversation. That's when the dialogue turned to the idea of dropping the same boss from a helicopter to straighten out his neck.

And that was it: Two minutes of discussion summarized in three paragraphs, a memo that made its way from the office of a district lieutenant to the desk of the deputy commissioner of the Baltimore Police Department. A piece of paper recounting a joke told in a crowded hotel room, which eventually ended up on my desk.

Of course, the three-paragraph brief didn't characterize the proposal to collect money to fund a contract killing as humorous, nor did the writer indicate anything amusing about dropping the intended victim out of a helicopter. The memo concluded the statements were a credible threat, a prelude to a murder.

But it wasn't just a joke that thrust me into a bizarre investigation that would alter my career path. No, it wasn't simply a few incendiary words that instigated the probe. It was the people doing the talking that transformed this mess into a full-blown excursion into the absurd.

Baltimore City Police. Cops.

The joke was told during a conversation among a dozen police officers holed up in Room 938. Cops worrying about losing their jobs... and blaming the boss. Of course, that "boss" happened to be then-Baltimore City Police Commissioner Donald D. Pomerleau.

That's right, sworn officers gathered in a hotel room in the middle of a tense labor battle plotting to kill the commissioner. Almost a dozen cops locked in an intense fight over job security and pay, alleged to have made threats deemed serious.

Actually, the anger, resentment and bitterness expressed in that small sliver of talk was symptomatic of the antipathy shared by hundreds of officers who were too pissed off, agitated, and, to be frank, too scared because they were out of work. Unfortunately, it was animosity expressed while someone was listening.

Bear in mind, this conversation took place during one of the most contentious labor battles in the history of Baltimore City Police. Four-hundred cops had taken part in a wildcat strike seeking better wages and job protections. And the same 400 had been suspended by Commissioner Pomerleau.

His reasoning?

Cops can't strike. And technically he was right.

So the police assembled in the hotel room were in a protracted and tense fight for their livelihood, a pitched battle which also included the added responsibility of saving the jobs of the 400 cops who had joined them in the strike.

But the real kicker in this whole tale of absurdity, the one detail that pushed this case onto the front pages of the *Baltimore Sun*, was the spy.

That's right, I believe to this day a top level commander planted a snitch in their midst — an officer working with top commanders to keep tabs on labor leaders, and report back. Whoever wrote the memo was listening too intently, and his recollection of the conversation was too precise to be providential. He was for all intents and purposes a double agent.

And you thought it was easy to be a cop.

Still, I don't know, and I probably never will know why command decided to plant a spy inside that hotel room. Yes, tension between then-Commissioner Pomerleau and the rank and file was palpable. City cops desperate for job protection and better pay had stepped out on a limb by walking out. The commissioner had struck back insisting that officers in a paramilitary organization didn't have the right to form a picket line.

The negotiations weren't going well to say the least. But still, spying on your own people?

I mean, I understand labor relations take on a whole different tenor when the workers carry guns and badges. Cops have unusual powers. They are indeed a paramilitary force, legally armed and ordained with arrest powers.

But a spy?

A STUBBORN MAN

As I've related several times in this book, Commissioner Pomerleau was an effective administrator, but he had a mean streak. He was an intimidating man with an imperious gaze and a gruff, no-nonsense demeanor. When you walked into his office, it was typical to have an eggshell moment. Don't utter an extra word, or make a casual observation, lest you end up in the cross-fire of one of his unrelenting critiques.

He was also a stubborn man who had suspended nearly 400 cops with a single stroke of the pen. A commissioner who threw down the gauntlet by taking the guns and badges of officers who joined a bitter wildcat strike, cops looking for a little extra pay and some assurances they couldn't be fired on the whim of a commander.

And I too had felt his ire.

Remember, he turned the tables on my probe of gambling on Pennsylvania Avenue. He was the commander who launched a very public investigation into my activities when a warrant disappeared and the case nearly fell apart. So I took a little satisfaction in the irony that the commissioner who swore I would never conduct a substantive investigation again, asked me to lead the probe.

What are the odds that the tables would turn so quickly? In the Book of Cop, faster than the blinking of an eye.

So when Deputy Commissioner Frank Battaglia invited me to his office for a briefing on the case, I didn't dwell on the past. In truth, I was actually focused on the contents of the memo authored by the spy, a memo which was scant on details.

First, there was little if any description of the state of mind of the officers involved in the alleged conversation. People like to bitch about the boss in imaginative ways. But there's a difference between a bitch session and hatching a scheme to off him. However, the mood, demeanor and disposition of the talkers is important, evidence that can point an investigation in the right direction.

I also had doubts about how the scheme was planned. Murder plots aren't hatched by committee. People who intend to kill usually keep the circle small. Why would cops planning on killing the commissioner discuss it while half a dozen witnesses wander in and out of the room?

Police may act dumb sometimes, but they're not stupid.

Still, my doubts about the facts didn't change my orders. The top cop wanted an investigation. I mean, I had the unexpected opportunity to redeem myself, and was eager to use it even if I was wary of the case itself.

And for the record, I didn't personally participate in the strike, but had sympathy for the men who did. As I recounted earlier in this book, there were minimal job protections for cops in my day. After I shot and killed a suspect I was suspended without pay. For several weeks I sat in purgatory, neither cop nor criminal, waiting for a judge to rule on my case. Thus I believe their justification for striking was legitimate.

It just wasn't my style. I was an investigator, not a labor leader.

You fight the battles that suit you.

LAUGHTER AND FORGETTING

As I pointed out in the chapter on the Pennsylvania Avenue gambling probe, investigating cops is dicey. Even a patrol officer knows the tricks of the trade when it comes to interrogation:

How to answer a question without answering it — Hint: Use "To the best of my knowledge..." and "I don't recall" as often as possible. How to keep the narrative consistent and believable. How to be vague about important facts, while offering up a rich assortment of irrelevant details to create the impression you're cooperating.

Still, when we started hauling in officers who were involved in the now nearly infamous conversation, their response was steely. Most of the cops I interviewed seemed dumbfounded, genuinely surprised to be sitting across the table from me. More than one was downright defiant.

"As far as I'm concerned, this is ridiculous," quipped one officer before I could even ask a single question.

But I was prepared for the bewildered; I was ready for pushback.

Think about it, who really believes they're guilty of a crime? And these guys were in the middle of a pitched labor battle; I'm sure they were cognizant this was more than just a criminal investigation. They were smart enough to know the probe could as easily have been aimed at retaliating against a group of labor leaders, rather than an investigation of cops involved in a murder plot.

That's why I decided to keep it simple. As I said before, I had too many doubts about the facts presented in the memo, and I was even less comfortable with the aforementioned motivation.

I couldn't help but question why in a city with hundreds of open murder cases on the books, was I wasting my time investigating an ambiguous threat culled from two minutes of seemingly incidental conversation. And why was I picked, out of hundreds of detectives, to head a probe at the behest of the man who for all intents and purposes had several years before declared my career as a detective over? Worst of all, why target the leaders of the strike with a seemingly flimsy murder-for-hire case that could end up aggravating an already tense situation? I mean, Pomerleau had already suspended nearly 400 cops. What did he want, a riot?

As you can see, I was in the theater of the absurd.

So with that in mind, I turned to the discipline which always bailed me out of dicey, politicized investigations. The set of precepts I always trusted to level the playing field and protect me and my fellow cops from the psychic abrasions of politics.

What I like to call the informal science of investigation. Techniques for compiling the truth about an alleged crime, gleaned from experience. Sort of an informal set of rules based upon my observations of human behavior, memory, and how we recall what we see.

It's an approach I liken to painting a picture from multiple perspectives. If you talk to enough witnesses, patterns emerge.

And I had plenty of witnesses— 16 to be exact.

The truth is, no two people tell a story exactly the same way; witnesses always conflict a bit. But during the course of recounting a particular incident or crime, certain common truisms are generally revealed. Simply put, there are always major plot points upon which nearly everyone agrees.

This is why I planned to ask the same set of questions to each cop — call it a pattern-recognition strategy — to obtain multiple versions of the same event gleaned by implementing a similar set of queries to create a relatively accurate picture.

Moreover there's a flip side to this technique.

If you want to figure out who's lying, use an identical strategy to unearth the anomalous. By asking the same set of questions, lying becomes self evident: The person creating a fiction often relays facts which jibe with the rest. So you have to dig deep to trip him up. It could be a tiny detail about timing, or sequence of events, or even the weather, but liars always get some crucial, commonly agreed-upon detail wrong.

Of course, for this technique to work, you have to keep some details under wraps. In other words, withhold some of the facts from the press. It's an often criticized tactic cops use, but the truth is, once all of the story is public, witnesses are indelibly corrupted.

Still, in this case, I had a small window.

It seemed inevitable the story of an investigation into a conspiracy to kill the police commissioner would get out: it was too hot to keep secret. I mean, amid a brutal contentious strike, a bunch of officers plot to kill the boss. And then an internal probe is launched to find the culprits? What reporter wouldn't want to write that headline?

So we hastily constructed a list of who was in the room that evening and brought each officer down to Headquarters one at a time.

And then, one by one, I sat down and questioned roughly 16 police officers who had either been in the room when the conversation occurred, or arrived shortly after it ended. And for each cop, I asked nearly the same series of questions. Simple, straightforward and direct, I didn't lead them, simply asked them to fill in the blanks.

And soon, a pattern did indeed emerge.

But first, the opening question — and the answers unembellished.

Officer "Smith": It is alleged you were involved in a conversation on July 15th, 1974 in Room 938 of the Lord Baltimore Hotel, about an alleged threat on the life of Commissioner Pomerleau. Is there anything you can tell me about this allegation?

Here are some of the more interesting answers:

"Someone said, 'Let's get a hit man.' This is when I said, 'Yeah, I'll take up a $10 collection.' It was just in jest."

"I do recall somebody saying something about a contract... I'm sure it was a joke."

"There was a lot of kidding around. An officer from the Central District had the TV on. He had The Price is Right on. He got down on his hands and knees and put his tongue out and said, 'Mr. Commissioner, may I blow you now, or wait awhile and blow you twice?'"

"There were several officers kidding around about fixing up the commissioner with their mother-in-laws."

"There were jokes going on... there was one about how the commissioner couldn't go back to Florida because there was a contract on him and he was just turned out of Tennessee."

"It was a big joke session and the guys were tired and I heard no one state deliberately that they were going to take the commissioner's life."

"Really truly, this is the most absurd and ridiculous thing I ever heard in my life."

"This has got to be the biggest joke I've ever been involved in."

And that was it, the best, most illustrative answers which emerged during my interrogation of 16 officers. Sixteen separate interviews peppered with denials, disavowals, and absolute surety of having no knowledge of what happened. An entire day and a half of questioning that yielded little but enlightening glimpses of how funny cops could and could not be.

Yes, there were some who recalled the discussion about raising money to hire an assassin. And several who were able to produce details about how the actual joke came about.

But even with the tacit admission that a joking threat had been made, there was little evidence that a murder-for-hire plot was in the offing. In fact, it was not even clear if the joke at the center of the controversy — a mock collection to pay for a hit man — had ever even been uttered.

The officer who the spy alleged had said it denied making the joke about the contract almost completely. And with the rest of the cops in the room either claiming they hadn't heard it or asserting the joke was just that, a joke, there just wasn't nearly enough evidence to proceed.

To make matters even dicier, halfway through the investigation, details of the incident made the front page of both the *Baltimore Sun* and *News American*.

"8 Quizzed in Pomerleau Death Plot," one of the headlines declared.

The story described how union leaders were shocked that a casual conversation inside a hotel room had been misconstrued as a death threat against the commissioner. The article also identified eight of the officers we had interviewed. For good measure the stories even revealed how the officers in the hotel room pooled 40 bucks to spend on booze — a healthy variety of hard liquor which they spent the night drinking, in-between trading jokes about icing Commissioner Pomerleau.

In reality, it was a circus, a sideshow which eclipsed the real event, the strike.

So I summarized my findings in two voluminous reports. My conclusion: it was a joke. Maybe a tasteless attempt at humor, maybe a few quips with an undertone of malice. But bottom line, there was no conspiracy among any of the officers to plot a murder.

The law is crystal clear: you need to do more than talk to be charged.

So that was the end of it — almost.

Because there was an interesting twist in this tale of a joke-turned-death-threat which emerged from the ashes, an unexpected turn of events that came from none other than Pomerleau himself.

Several days after I completed the interviews, I presented the results of my investigation to the commissioner. As usual, Pomerleau was aloof and laser-focused. Still, he seemed unimpressed with my conclusions. It was as if my findings were at that moment an afterthought.

In fact, sitting in front of his desk, waiting as he meditated on my findings, I thought he would likely mete out administrative punishment against the officers involved. Internal charges that would allow him to save face while distracting from the fact that this entire incident had been, well, absurd.

A police commissioner has pretty much absolute discretion to charge officers administratively. Internal sanctions that aren't necessarily criminal, but can just as easily end an officer's career.

To make matters worse for the officers under fire, the charges were based solely upon what's known as general orders, a book of procedures that govern everything from how to wear a uniform to how to behave when you're sitting in your backyard drinking a beer. Believe me, it's a relatively flexible code that can be tailored to the needs of any commander seeking to dress down a subordinate, regardless of the circumstance.

But as I sat in that chair in Commissioner Pomerleau's office feeling a little antsy, something unexpected happened. The hard-ass, tough as nails administrator shook his head and set my report aside. He looked straight at me, the same unfettered glare that preceded his death knell on my career as an investigator.

"I guess these men have been through enough," he said. "This is over, let's put it to rest."

I was stunned. Frankly, I didn't know what to say, it was the last thing I expected to hear. He hardly blinked before dismissing me with the wave of a hand.

"Yes, sir," I answered.

And so that was it. Instead of plotting to put these men permanently out on the street, Pomerleau had gone soft.

I sort of wish I could have asked him what prompted this unexpected act of mercy. To this day, I still wonder why he chose to de-escalate.

Maybe he was wise enough to know allegations that a handful of drunk cops had hatched a plot to kill him was indeed ridiculous. Or maybe he really was feeling compassionate. Better still, perhaps he was already planning to re-hire all the officers and settle a strike that had set the entire city on edge.

In the end, it could have been the pragmatic administrator who made the call, rather than the ill-tempered megalomaniac.

However the truth is, I didn't really want to ask. Or want to know.

But it's also possible the commissioner recognized the force which buffets all cops, and decided it was futile to push the issue further. Maybe he was smart enough to acknowledge the tide of confusion and chaos driving the whole bizarre sequence of events toward a potentially bad ending.

Even commissioners aren't immune to it. I know I never was.

The curse of the absurd.

EPILOGUE

The Purpose of This Book

YOU CAN'T STOP MURDER

On the preceding pages I have tried to describe and analyze the trials and tribulations of being a cop, in particular in the City of Baltimore. Also the many satisfactions that come with the knowledge of having performed a job well done.

Unfortunately You Can't Stop Murder, as I've reiterated time and again on these pages. The best you can hope for is to lessen its frequency and impact.

It is my hope however that my experiences good and bad will help guide present and future police officers — not just in Baltimore, but everywhere — to be the best cops they can possibly be. And to enable Baltimore to live up to its current nickname: Charm City.

Also to help set the Baltimore Police Department on a straight and narrow course to become the best of its kind in America... and the world.

The good people of Charm City deserve nothing less.

Made in the USA
Columbia, SC
19 February 2018